KU-175-001

PUFFIN BOOKS

SURVIVE!

OCEAN TERROR

The *Carolina* was being tossed about like driftwood by the whirling, swirling sea.

Suddenly the boat swung side-on to the waves and the whole vessel went over at a sharp angle yet again. Gina snatched at the table and jammed her knees under it. Scott grabbed on to her midriff …

Gina shouted out. 'We're sinking, we're sinking!'

Scott could barely see her now, but he caught the unmistakable sound of fear in her voice.

'No!' Scott yelled as they hung on to each other. 'This boat is self-righting! Come on! Don't let's lose it!'

Despite his rallying cry, his body was shuddering with ripples of cold fear.

Scott's heart pounded. He looked into the abyss outside. Are we sinking? he thought.

SURVIVE!

OCEAN TERROR

Jack Dillon

PUFFIN BOOKS

Special thanks to David Clayton and Ian Locke
Additional thanks to John Le Quesne
for his expert help

PUFFIN BOOKS

Published by the Penguin Group
Penguin Books Ltd, 27 Wrights Lane, London W8 5TZ, England
Penguin Putnam Inc., 375 Hudson Street, New York, New York 10014, USA
Penguin Books Australia Ltd, Ringwood, Victoria, Australia
Penguin Books Canada Ltd, 10 Alcorn Avenue, Toronto, Ontario, Canada M4V 3B2
Penguin Books (NZ) Ltd, Private Bag 102902, NSMC, Auckland, New Zealand

On the World Wide Web at: www.penguin.com

Penguin Books Ltd, Registered Offices: Harmondsworth, Middlesex, England

First published 2000
1 3 5 7 9 10 8 6 4 2

Text copyright © Working Partners Ltd, 2000
All rights reserved

The moral right of the author has been asserted

Set in Bembo

Made and printed in England by Clays Ltd, St Ives plc

Except in the United States of America, this book is sold subject to the condition that
it shall not, by way of trade or otherwise, be lent, re-sold, hired out, or otherwise
circulated without the publisher's prior consent in any form of binding or cover other
than that in which it is published and without a similar condition including this
condition being imposed on the subsequent purchaser

British Library Cataloguing in Publication Data
A CIP catalogue record for this book is available from the British Library

ISBN 0–141–30444–8

CHAPTER ONE

The helicopter chattered noisily over the warm, blue Caribbean Sea. Inside it, Scott Rogan ran a hand through his blond hair and smiled across at his sister, Gina.

She didn't notice. She didn't seem able to take her eyes off the silver shoals that wheeled and turned, catching the light like a million diamonds, in the clear waters below. 'Wow! Just look at that, Scott!' she said, pointing down again at the massive expanse of water, her face glowing.

Scott too was impressed by the ocean vista; it took his breath away. His heart was thumping at the prospect of their holiday adventure ahead. They were now clear of Puerto Rico and were heading south-east for Tortola in the British Virgin Islands.

'Look!' Gina could hardly sit still. 'A shark!'

Scott grinned and glanced down at a large, dark shape moving slowly through the masses of small fish.

'I'd like to get a few close-up photos of that,' said Gina. Her underwater camera was ready in her pack and Scott knew she couldn't wait to use it.

Scott leaned back, overwhelmed by the intensity of the view. 'What shall we do first, Gina? Scuba dive? Water ski?'

'Plenty of time for everything, folks,' their uncle, Clancy Stone, bellowed above the sound of the whirring helicopter blades. 'But first let's get to Tortola and see if the *Carolina* has made it down from Nassau. Otherwise we won't be going anywhere!' Clancy was a great sun-tanned bear of a man and was sitting up front, next to the pilot. His leathery skin, bright green eyes and hair flecked with grey made him look every inch the weather-beaten sailor.

The helicopter was taking Scott, Gina and their uncle to Roadtown, where Clancy planned to pick up his boat. From there they would sail along the outlying string of islands and then beyond, into the Atlantic Ocean itself.

Scott couldn't wait. Over the last few years he had sailed several smaller boats: every summer they had gone to their gran's home near Cape Cod. There, Gina had dived and photographed marine life, while Scott had been out in his dinghy. However, nothing he'd ever done up there quite matched the thrill he felt now about this trip. He'd never actually seen the *Carolina* for real, but just the photos of her really excited him.

Clancy pointed out to sea. 'Looking good out there, Jim. Plenty of big ones!' he said to the pilot.

'There's always good fishing here,' Jim replied. 'Must keep an eye out for the weather, though – this being July and all. It's been a bad season. Very bad.'

'Yeah, I know. Been out there in a few big blows myself.' Clancy had told Scott and Gina about some of the big storms he'd experienced.

January and February were the best months for these waters but, unfortunately, he had been working in Mexico then. He'd been promising Scott and Gina a sailing trip for ages, and they had finally managed to fix a date after school had finished for the summer.

'Anyway, it's looking OK right now,' Clancy

said reassuringly. 'The storm track is way, way to the south-west, according to the radio.'

The early-morning sun was blazing in the clear sky and there wasn't a cloud in sight.

Below, Scott noticed the dark line of a reef and more sparkling shoals of fish. The water was so clear he thought he could see right down to the sea-bed.

The helicopter zoomed over several small islands. Some were just patches of white sand, no bigger than a volleyball court; others were dotted with small fishing huts. In between were more reefs, and it was clear that to sail in these waters you'd have to know what you were doing. A reef could easily tear open the hull of a boat, no matter how big it was.

Scott glanced at Clancy. His uncle had been in the oil business for twenty-five years and had travelled all over the world: Alaska, Mexico, the Gulf, Borneo. He'd been there, done it, seen it and probably eaten it. He never seemed to back away from a challenge. Scott sometimes thought that he was a frustrated explorer, and he could imagine him canoeing solo down the Amazon or the Congo with just a bunch of bananas and bottle of whisky to keep him going. He looked like a survivor, used to hard knocks.

He was very different from Scott's dad, another oil man. He had been a quiet, studious man; he had died in a car crash a couple of years ago when Scott was thirteen and Gina a year younger. Their mother had been lucky to survive, and she still hadn't fully recovered emotionally. Her elder brother, their Uncle Clancy, had been a fantastic help. Scott was amazed how much Clancy had done to put their lives back together again.

Sailing was Clancy's passion and he took to the waves whenever his job allowed him to. However, in the last two years he had had very little free time for sailing. This trip was the first chance Clancy had had to relax for a while, as well as being a dream trip for Scott and Gina. They were looking forward to it immensely and were determined that their uncle would also enjoy himself.

Scott looked out around the islands and spotted a change in colour on the water. Beyond the line of reefs, the sea was dark and flat. 'How deep is it out there?' he asked.

'Two thousand metres plus, even close in to the islands,' Jim replied. 'Eight thousand metres in the Puerto Rico Trench that we've just passed.'

'Wow, that's five miles deep!' Scott was

excited by the idea. 'You could sink a whole town in there!'

'Yep, and that's where we're going later,' Clancy grinned. 'Got to cross it on the way back up to Bimini to meet your mom and gran. We'll be out there soon, guys.'

The islands were becoming more frequent as the helicopter headed south, out of the direct glare of the sun. Now they could see boats of all kinds moored in little bays along the way; one huge white craft was close to a massive reef.

'See that?' said the pilot, nodding his head towards the boat. 'Stupid. His anchor-chain will rake along that reef and smash the coral. Ten years of that, and you've got no coral left.'

'Ten years? That's disgusting!' Gina gasped. 'It can take a thousand years for a reef to form.'

Scott admired his sister's passion for the natural world. At one time Scott had been a little jealous of Gina. She was an excellent athlete and swimmer; everything seemed so effortless for her. Sparks had flown between her and Scott when they were younger, but the accident had changed all that. Now they kept an eye out for each other without making a big deal out of it. Sometimes when they exchanged glances they both knew what the other was thinking without a word passing between them.

Scott looked at his watch. 'How long before we land, Jim?'

The pilot glanced at his dials. 'Ten minutes,' he said. 'We'll swing round the east side of Tortola, over Jost Van Dyke, and land at Beef Island.'

'Hey! Look at that!' Scott pointed to a small, white powerboat that was cutting a wide 'V' of wake with its sharp bow as it flew at great speed over the water below.

'They're really moving!' Gina said enthusiastically. 'Why are they in such a hurry?'

Clancy looked down. 'Maybe it's Customs on the lookout for smugglers,' he suggested. 'Who knows?'

'They don't have pirates and smugglers now, surely?' Gina asked.

'Not any of your Long John Silver stuff, no,' said the pilot. 'Certainly not rum and pieces-of-eight and treasure chests. These days it's drugs, I'm afraid – probably brought in from South America.'

Scott watched the boat disappear behind them out of sight. 'I read in one of the guidebooks that there's treasure out there. The book said that those pirate guys in the old days didn't trust anybody. They'd just try to remember special rocks and stuff where they buried the treasure, and then drew maps with them on.'

'Mmm – maybe!' Clancy laughed.

Gina's eyes widened. 'Are there any wrecks?' she asked.

'Cuba's the place for wrecks,' said the pilot. 'Off Havana there are whole galleons.'

'There!' Clancy said suddenly. 'That's where our trip really begins – Tortola.'

Up ahead Scott saw the pointed cone of a volcanic island on the horizon. 'I just can't wait!' In his mind, Scott could already feel the warm water all round him.

'We'll be there in five minutes,' Jim said.

'Better get ready, then,' said Gina, checking the gear in her rucksack.

The silver helicopter swooped down like a great dragonfly over the huge cone of the volcano. Below, dozens of boats criss-crossed the channels: sailboats, cruisers, speedboats, sail boards, water skiers and fishing boats. To the left was the sugary sand of Jost Van Dyke Island. Beyond the cone to the right was Roadtown harbour, full of expensive yachts and vivid-coloured boats of every size and shape. Ahead was the little airport at Beef Island, connected to Tortola by a narrow causeway. Tortola was the largest island in the group and Roadtown was the main port.

Minutes later, the wind blasted Scott's hair back as he ducked under the helicopter's whirling blades on the landing pad. He grinned as he walked clear of the turbulence and felt the silky Caribbean air on his face. This is the life! he thought.

CHAPTER TWO

As the blades swished to a halt, Scott and Gina walked slowly away towards the Customs Office.

Scott sniffed the air. 'This is great!' he said, and then he breathed in deeply. He loved the smell of the ocean. His eyes scanned the boats out in the channel. There were some real beauties there. Finally, he turned to focus on the cone of the volcano that towered into the blue sky way above the small airport building.

Gina followed Scott's gaze upwards. 'Wow! That's steep! I suppose it really *is* dead?'

'They wouldn't build right below if it wasn't, would they?' Scott said. 'Maybe we'll have time to explore it later.'

'Doubt it,' said Clancy, coming up behind them. 'It's bigger than you think. Going up there would take the best part of a day, and there's so much to see out in the islands.' Then Clancy hesitated. He clearly didn't want to railroad them. 'I mean … you can go up there if you really want …'

'No,' Gina said. 'Let's get out to sea. That's what we've really been looking forward to. I can't wait to get my flippers on and my camera working.'

They were through Customs in no time at all.

Clancy, Scott and Gina made their way towards the nearest car park, where a blue jeep was waiting for them with a Caribbean guy leaning on it. He was youngish, in his thirties, and looked cool in a pale-blue shirt, New York Mets baseball cap and brilliant purple shorts. When he stood up straight he towered over Scott like a basketball player.

'How did the trip down from Nassau go, Orlando?' Clancy called.

Clancy had got Orlando and Sam, two local sailors, to bring the *Carolina* down from her regular berth in the Bahamas. They were going to help crew the boat during their sailing trip.

'Not too bad!' the man said, giving Clancy

11

a bear hug and an exaggerated high five. He nodded and smiled at Scott and Gina. 'Sam said he had one or two little things to sort. You know boats – they always want a little more of your attention! Sam will explain.'

'I often get local sailors to move the boat about,' Clancy explained to Scott and Gina as they loaded up the jeep with their bags. 'That way you can just fly out and sail from anywhere you like. It's better than sailing out from the same home port all the time.' He turned back to Orlando. 'Are we all set, though? We can sail straight away, right?' Clancy didn't go in for small talk.

'Well … Sam thinks so, but I'd be happier if you could check her out yourself. Maybe just down the channel and back.'

'Sure,' Clancy said. 'Tell you what,' he added, motioning to everyone to get in the jeep, 'let's just get on down to Roadtown, and then we'll sort out what we're doing when we arrive.'

The road from the airport snaked in and out, with the harbour on one side and great wooded slopes on the other.

Scott marvelled at the variety of local fishing boats. People were unloading catches, washing decks, mending nets and preparing to sail. They were singing, whistling, laughing and joking. The place was buzzing with life.

Further on were the moorings for pleasure boats: yachts and cruisers, sloops and catamarans. The masts of the boats formed a chaotic forest, stretching right out into the channel.

Now they entered the town itself, which was a busy mix of new and old buildings. Scott could see that there were several luxury hotels and bars, but behind them, cut off now from the sea, were older, wooden houses. As Scott watched the boats, Gina looked down the side streets. It was a different world from the modern suburbs of upper New York State where they had lived all their lives. Here, there was history all around them.

Scott noticed that Clancy was excited too. His uncle was looking eagerly across at the mass of boats and his fingers drummed a rapid rhythm as they drove.

'Hey, it's getting cloudy!' Gina said suddenly, looking up at the sky.

Scott gave the sky a glance too.

'It's just the season,' Clancy explained. 'Gets real hot. Clouds up in the afternoon and rains. Half an hour later, the sun's blasting away again.'

Scott noticed that Clancy wasn't looking at Gina as he spoke. His eyes were cutting across the water. Scott turned to see what his uncle was looking at. 'Hey, the *Carolina*!'

There she was: white and gleaming, appearing bigger and more beautiful than he had imagined.

Scott was stunned. The jeep pulled up and Scott leapt out. He ran to the yacht and touched the sleek white hull. For once, words failed him. 'It's really … Wow!'

Clancy's chest seemed to puff out as he touched Scott's shoulder before jumping aboard. He began to tell them more about the boat. 'She's a forty-nine-foot sloop, three cabins, state-of-the-art offshore cruiser, sixty-three horse-power and a real wave-buster. Range: thirteen hundred miles.'

Scott was impressed. His eyes ran up the surprisingly tall mast, topped by a radar aerial. Although the mast was slender, Scott got an overall impression of sleekness and power from the boat herself. The cockpit was located just abaft of centre; a windscreen shielded it and a metal guard-rail surrounding it glittered. She was ready for big seas. Behind, Scott saw the inflatable life-raft in its fittings and, right at the stern, little steps led down to where an inshore dinghy bobbed on the water.

'It's just fantastic!' gasped Gina, standing on the deck and doing a little twirl around to try and take everything in.

'Yes, I love her too!' Clancy smiled. He strode up to the cockpit and caressed the wheel gently.

Just then, another local guy, who Scott took to be Sam, appeared on the deck from below. He was a little butterball of a man, bursting out of his cherry-red shirt and blue cotton trousers.

Sam waved casually but did not smile. 'Hello, Mr Stone,' he said.

'Hi, Sam,' Clancy said.

Within minutes, they had loaded the gear on board and Scott was sitting at the helm, stroking the wheel as if it was a piece of antique furniture.

Gina went down to the cabins. 'Scott, just look at this!' he heard, moments later.

Scott jumped nimbly down below to find himself in a comfortable saloon with stylish curtains, a large table and bookshelves all round. Everything was crafted in teak with brass fittings.

'Yes!' he enthused. Of course, he had been round boats like this before – when he had painted boats for pocket money and cleared docks down near Gran's at Cape Rock. But those boats belonged to strangers. Clancy was family and Scott immediately felt at home.

Gina peered out through the ports, examined the books on the shelves, then moved on to her cabin. Scott lay back on a bench seat to test it. He was good at relaxing!

Gina disturbed his temporary rest. 'Look at this!' She was one surprise ahead of him. He hauled himself up to inspect the ultra-comfortable cabins.

Right away he got busy, stowing his gear in the spacious double berth he was to share with Gina. The bunks were luxurious. Gina checked her photographic gear carefully. By the time they were out at sea, it would be too late to replace anything or buy any new equipment.

'I didn't expect it to be like this!' said Gina.

Scott just grinned and gave her a playful punch on the arm. 'This is the life, eh?'

A few moments later, Orlando came down to find them.

'This …' he said, 'is my speciality – the galley – although we'll all share some of the work.' The galley kitchen was gleaming stainless steel, compact and with everything easily accessible.

Scott and Gina didn't mind work. Their parents had never spoilt them and they'd both had regular summer jobs. Scott had had his boatyard job and Gina had helped teach young children to swim at summer camp. She had bought her undersea camera with the money she had earned.

Gina pointed to Scott. 'Watch him when it's his turn to cook, Orlando. He eats faster than he cooks.'

Orlando grinned.

'All good chefs taste their own food,' Scott protested. 'I thought everyone knew that!'

Gina just laughed.

But her laughter was cut short by the sound of raised voices on deck.

Clancy wasn't the loud type, but his voice had an edge to it. 'Where are you going?' he asked.

'I'm going to Cartagena on the *Corpus Christi*,' Scott heard Sam reply. 'We sail tonight.'

'Colombia? Tonight? You could have told us before this!'

By this time, Scott was in the cockpit, where he saw Sam looking sheepish, staring at his feet and shuffling about. Clancy's face was bright red.

'Sorry, Mr Stone. It's five weeks' work. I'd stay for another five hundred.'

'No way!' Clancy snapped and, wasting no more time, pointed to the dock. 'Goodbye, Sam. Thanks for everything,' he added sarcastically.

The little man stomped off up the steps and was gone.

Orlando stood on the deck with his baseball cap in his hand and scratched his head. 'Man! That's all we need.'

'We'll still sail tonight,' Clancy declared. 'We'll go down along the outer islands, then up to Bimini as planned. But first we'll try her out down Drake Channel just to be sure everything's OK.'

Scott took this all in. He knew enough about sailing to know that, with all its electrics, there was usually no problem crewing a boat like this with four hands aboard rather than five.

'We don't need him, do we, Orlando?' Clancy asked.

Orlando smiled. 'No – sirree!'

'Tell you what, I'll give you a bonus for all the extra work,' Clancy said.

'No prob-lem!' Orlando's grin lit up his face!

Scott and Gina smiled.

Clancy still looked a little annoyed with Sam. He turned to Scott and Gina. 'Me and Orlando have got some work to do. How about you two taking a stroll around the harbour, check out the local life? Hmm, it's a little after two. See you around four, OK?'

Scott was caught between asking if he could help and getting a closer look at the other boats in Nanny Cay Marina. However, he couldn't very well leave Gina on her own in a new port, and he had noticed that there were loads of specialist chandlers and scuba shops, selling really cool leisure gear. It was definitely his kind of place.

They watched the *Carolina* depart and headed for the stores. However, when Scott saw some of the prices he whistled, and soon they were heading for the jetty that led out to where the water was deeper. There the big boats, the *super* boats, were moored.

On their way, they passed four locals playing cards outside a bar. One laughed, showing a mouthful of broken teeth. Another had a bright green bandanna round his neck.

'They look like pirates!' Gina whispered conspiratorially. One of the men glanced up and gave her an evil grin. She moved away quickly.

As they walked out along a wooden jetty, an American voice, not very different from their own, rang out. 'I spy tourists!'

The words made them look around, then down. A tall, sun-tanned boy with bleached hair sat, grinning up at them, in a dinghy below. He was wearing wraparound mirrored shades and baggy Bermuda shorts sporting a crazy zebra pattern.

'Hey! What's with this "tourist" stuff?' Scott said jokily. 'And have you got a licence for those shorts?'

'Hi,' said the zebra boy. 'I'm Cy Jensen.'

'Do you live here?' Scott asked. The boy looked relaxed and very much part of the local scene.

'No, but when school's on vacation I live there.' He pointed over his shoulder at one of the yachts moored way out. 'Sometimes we're over at Puerto Mogan in the Canaries. Sometimes it's Rio. Sometimes here. Home's Rhode Island, USA.'

'We spend most summers down at Cape Cod,' Gina said.

'Nice place! So we're almost neighbours then! Or would be – if I was ever there in summer! We've got a great boat, a seventy-foot ketch. Good crew, too. Fancy looking her over? Dad and the rest are ashore – it's some guy's birthday and I'm not invited!'

A few seconds later, the outboard motor on the dinghy was chugging and they were heading out over blue water for Cy's yacht, beyond the clutter of the moorings. The southern sky was a mass of fluffy cloud which seemed to climb and darken by the minute. It was pushing three o'clock now. The hazy sun was still very high overhead. However, in spite of the haze, Scott felt its hot rays on his neck. There was no sign of a cooling breeze.

'There she is,' said the other boy, pointing, 'that's the *Swordfish*, our yacht.'

Scott just goggled. 'That's some boat!'

'You'd better believe it!' Cy said. 'She can make it to Europe in fifteen days.'

'That's flying!' Scott nodded in appreciation.

Scott thought about the *Swordfish*, then about the *Carolina*. He looked back across the harbour. Cy's ketch dwarfed their sloop.

Scott took in the long lines of the ketch, with its rear cockpit and high safety rail right round the outside of the deck. It was quite a different style from a sloop, a longer boat with a mizzen mast and a sharper bow to cut big waves more cleanly.

Soon, they were out of the inflatable and on

board the *Swordfish*. Cy immediately took them for a conducted tour down below.

Below decks, it was even more luxurious than the *Carolina*, and bigger too. It was a ten-berth at least, and there were other things that also surprised Scott and Gina.

'It's got central heating!' Gina gasped.

'Yeah, Dad had it customized. My family originally came from Denmark, so he fancies himself as a Viking, sailing in northern waters. We even got up to Greenland and Iceland one time!'

'I don't believe this – a washing machine!' Scott laughed, peering round a corner.

'What's this …?' Gina asked, unable to believe her eyes.

'Looks like an old electric organ!' Scott added.

Cy held his hands up in denial.

'Hey, don't look at me, guys. That's Dad's toy. You're lucky – I have to stay here and listen to him! You can't escape at sea like you can at home!'

Scott was gazing about him. 'This is one big ship! Say, you haven't got a bowling alley hidden round here someplace, have you?'

'Sorry, pal!' Cy smiled. 'Want to see the controls – the electrics?'

Once again, the sight was impressive.

Scott checked out the radio. Gina went to look at the green screen. 'What's this?' she asked.

'Weather radar. Take a look.'

Cy fiddled with a keyboard and the screen showed the whole of the Caribbean. There were a number of larger swirls of cloud.

'See those?' he said. 'They're cyclones, storm tracks. Been a lot around lately.'

'Hurricanes?' Scott queried.

Gina cut in. 'There's more than one kind of storm, Scott.'

'Yeah,' Cy smiled. 'Storms go from Cat one to Cat five. Hurricanes are four or five. We've got maybe a Cat one coming this way. The real bad stuff seems to be down there. Off Panama maybe – or over round Cartagena or Aruba. Hundreds of miles away.'

Gina and Scott exchanged anxious glances.

'Don't worry about storms,' Cy said, 'these boats are made to take them.'

Just then there was a sudden heavy pattering on the deck.

'It's raining!' Gina said. 'But there's no storm around here on your screen!'

'You're right,' Cy said. 'It's only convectional rain. It happens every day in the tropics.'

Scott noticed a fresh bunch of bananas on a table. Cy saw him eyeing the fruit. 'Help yourself,' he offered. 'I've got some swordfish steaks too, if you're really hungry.'

Gina just laughed. 'Cy, you might live to regret that invitation. Scott is always ready for food!'

'But I'm a growing boy!' Scott protested.

'More like a car crusher at lunchtime. He could eat for America!' his sister added.

An hour later, when they'd eaten their fill, they went up on deck again. Now, the sky was a clear blue and bright sunlight gleamed off the great yacht. Scott and Gina checked out a whole range of state-of-the-art scuba gear. They even had jet skis!

'Guess we'd better get going,' Scott said. 'Clancy will be expecting us back.'

'Already?' Gina asked.

'It's way past four.' Scott checked his Seamaster watch, then peered into the sunlight. 'See.' As he pointed, the *Carolina* was cruising back down the channel towards the moorings.

'Yours?' Cy asked. Scott nodded. 'Great boat,' the other boy added.

As Cy steered the dinghy back to the

Carolina, he spoke to the other two about their holiday plans. 'Where are you headed?' he asked.

'Rainbow Cay, Three Parrots, Dead Man's Cove, down that way,' Scott said.

'Us too! See you over there maybe!'

When Cy dropped them off at the quayside, Scott and Gina saw that Clancy and Orlando had spotted them. Gina waved.

'See you around!' Cy shouted as he cruised away.

'Sure thing!' Scott replied. 'Thanks for lunch.'

Gina stood watching Cy's boat returning to the ketch.

Scott was ready for action and he hustled along the jetty to the *Carolina*. Clancy was standing, waiting, in the cockpit.

'Are we going to be delayed?' Scott asked Clancy, when he'd climbed on deck.

'No way,' Clancy said. 'We're almost ready now. Just a few bits and pieces to sort out, then we're off.'

Gina grinned at Scott. 'Yes!' they said together, giving each other high fives.

Far out from harbour, where there was less shelter, foam was kicking up from a reef and the anchored boats rocked and bobbed. The trees on the point of land beyond the volcano flapped in the wind that had sprung up since the rain. Scott looked up. Sure, the sun was hot enough – but was the sky quite so blue on the southern horizon?

While Gina settled down on the deck to sunbathe, down below on his bunk Scott looked at sea charts. The crossing to the Bahamas was a long stretch without land. But the boat was rock solid and could go 1,300 miles without refuelling. He thought of the swirls on the storm radar, but then he thought again about what Cy had told them: that in summer there are always storm tracks somewhere in the Caribbean. If you waited for a clear screen you'd never sail! Clancy was experienced and so was Orlando and, if he was honest with himself, the prospect of big seas gave Scott a thrill – he had already tried white-water canoeing and had loved the adrenalin rush.

He sat back, daydreaming about the journey ahead, and after a while he began to doze on his bunk.

Suddenly, the diesel engine underneath him kicked into life and the sloop began to cruise steadily out into the channel. Yes! They were moving!

Clancy shouted up above. 'Half-revs? OK?'

'OK,' said Orlando at the wheel.

'Well, whaddya know!' Clancy was looking back towards the port. Scott came up on deck to join him.

A little fat figure in a cherry-red shirt stood watching from the deck of a big blue yacht. It was Sam Pacifico and he was shaking his head. Maybe he'd seen the weather forecast for Cartagena and realized that he'd had the chance of a fun trip and had blown it.

Gina waved, but the sailor turned away.

It's your loss, Sam, Scott thought, as they cruised steadily out into the channel towards the open sea.

CHAPTER THREE

As the *Carolina* cleared the moorings, Scott and Gina got a view of the whole of Drake Channel, a mile-wide funnel leading out into the ocean. All along its sides were smaller islands with boats of various sizes at anchor. It was after six and the sun was starting to sink in the west. The channel side of the volcanic islands was starting to melt into hazy purple shadow against the blaze of orange sky.

Scott sat at the bow and studied the passing boats. 'Can I take a turn at the helm?' he asked, the wind blowing his hair back.

Orlando glanced at Clancy, who was checking the safety gear behind him. 'Not right here, Scott. Too much traffic on these channels,' Clancy said. 'We've got to weave our way through all this stuff first.' He pointed to a sailboard that was cutting across, dangerously close to another yacht. 'And watch out for idiots like that guy!'

After twenty minutes more, Orlando turned to Clancy. 'Anchor up at Rainbow Cay? Then, maybe eat? That's better than trying to make Three Parrot Island after dark.' He was looking at the falling sun.

Night was coming, Scott thought, and the south-west sky was beginning to cloud up too.

'Open her up a bit and see how we go,' Clancy said. 'We don't need to decide yet.'

'Sure thing,' Orlando replied.

The big engine thundered louder and Orlando steered on.

By seven, the sun was riding low on the western horizon and the eastern sky was black.

'Watch for the "green flash" as the sun dips out of sight,' Gina said.

'OK,' Scott replied.

Soon the sun looked as though it was balanced on the rim of the world, then, bit by bit, it eased out of sight. At the exact moment it disappeared, Scott's eyes played a trick and for a split second the line of the horizon was green. Now an orange glow lit the sea. Scott stood silently, taking it all in.

Scott didn't quite have Gina's eye for natural beauty, but the stunning sunset, the great empty sea and Clancy's kindness had all got to him. He'd spent too long recently bottling up his emotions by always trying to stay cheerful for his mom and 'little' sister. He thought about his dad. Suddenly he missed him a huge amount all over again. He felt hands on his shoulders, and he turned to see the same thoughts reflected in Gina's moist eyes. 'I know,' she said and gave him a hug. She had obviously been watching him closely.

A narrow, deserted island appeared ahead. Beyond it, to the west, Scott could see anchor lights.

'Rainbow Cay!' Orlando called to Clancy, who was below deck. 'We got company on the other side of the island. Shall we move on?'

'No, this'll do,' Clancy said. 'Just bring us in a bit closer, then anchor up.'

A minute or two later, Orlando furled the sails with the power winch and then released the anchor. Apart from the swish of the breeze and the slap of the water, the world was suddenly silent.

'Tuna OK for you guys tonight?' Orlando said, as he headed for the galley, still grinning.

'You want any help?' Scott shouted, snapping out of his melancholy.

'No, this one's all prepared,' Orlando said, returning with three long cool drinks. 'You guys chill out on deck.'

Soon the smell of tuna steaks and frying onions wafted up from the galley below.

Scott looked down at the dark waters running by, at the ominous shapes of the islands and the great sea beyond. There might be other boats around, he thought, but really you're alone out here.

Suddenly, something was coming. The roar of a powerful engine moving fast up the channel was closing on them by the second. They couldn't see it because it was running, dangerously, without lights. Orlando had made sure they had *their* white anchor lights on, of course, but who could be moving at that speed in the dark?

WHOOoosssshhh! The black speedboat passed within a hundred metres of their starboard side. Then it powered away out of sight.

'Why hasn't it got any lights on?' Gina demanded.

Orlando had come up on deck as the

Carolina jumped and skipped in the wash from the other boat. 'Don't know. Don't want to know!' he said.

'But he could have hit us!' Scott said indignantly.

'No way,' Orlando replied. 'Got night sights, see? Also, he'll know this place like the back of his hand.'

'Who was it?' Gina wanted to know.

'I really don't know,' Orlando said.

He didn't say anything more about the mysterious craft, but the silence was soon cut short by the sound of yet another powerful engine.

Scott looked towards the sound. Another boat, this one carrying bright lights, was heading out of the port – fast. Seconds later she swept by, rocking them even more roughly with her wake.

'They're really moving,' Gina commented.

'Yeah, they looked like the good guys!' Orlando laughed. 'No use, though. If the black boat did have contraband on board, it'll be over the side before the police get anywhere near.'

Scott felt cold inside and a bit more vulnerable than he had before. It was all right just talking about things happening out here. Now he had seen the reality.

But Orlando's feast cheered him up somewhat. The tuna, bread and salad was delicious and every morsel was quickly eaten. Orlando really knew how to cook.

As soon as everything was cleared away, Orlando produced a guitar and, before long, a reggae beat echoed out across the waters.

Clancy slipped below deck, but he returned shortly afterwards, frowning a little.

Gina looked up. Overhead, the sky had been as clear as anything, with the stars going on for ever, but now wispy clouds were running fast from the south-west.

Scott noticed that the boat was rocking and bucking more. He looked south and realized that he couldn't see the stars at all in that direction. Then he saw what Clancy must also have noticed.

His uncle was soon on the weather radar.

Orlando stopped playing. 'What does the weather look like, Clancy?'

'It's a bit uncertain. It depends on the way the weather front develops. Could be nothing, could be a Cat two.'

Orlando looked all around him. 'I've got a feeling that it's all going to get bumpy some time soon.'

Soon Gina went down below deck to her

bunk, but Scott didn't follow her. The niggling worries flitting through his mind drove out any immediate thoughts of sleep. He sat on the steps at the stern of the boat. Seeing the strength of the current pulling at the sloop, he fixed a line from his light safety harness to the rail, aft of the cockpit, before trailing his feet in the water. He felt uneasy.

What's the matter with me? There's nothing to be scared of, he thought, as he looked at the distant lights of boats moored beyond the island. His mind flew from the guys in the speedboat to the storm warning, and then to the dark waters into which he was dangling his feet. The image of a shark flashed into his mind. Something touched his foot and he quickly whipped his feet out of the warm sea.

This is silly! he thought to himself. Clancy knows what he's doing. Orlando is cool. We're only offshore, not in the middle of the Atlantic! But he just couldn't shake off the bad vibes he had. Come on, Scott, come on! he thought. You've come a long way in two years. You're not a kid any more. You can't lose it now.

The boat lights flickered and went out. Was something wrong with the electrics? No, the lights came back on in a second. It couldn't be anything much, could it?

Scott turned when he heard somebody behind him. 'Problems?'

'No. But even if we did have, we've got reserve power,' Clancy said.

The wind was starting to pick up a bit, and now the clouds were really racing across the stars above as Clancy eased himself down on to the step alongside him. He was even smiling.

'It's a big world out there, isn't it?' Clancy said, echoing Scott's feelings.

'Darkness and silence bother me sometimes,' Scott admitted.

'You and me both!' Clancy said. 'You get used to it, though. The way you get used to all the noise in LA or New York.'

'Sometimes I reckon I think too much,' said Scott.

'I know …' Clancy put his arm round Scott's shoulders '… but you're doing great, just great. Your dad would be proud of you.'

'Thanks, Clancy. For everything.'

'My pleasure.'

They stood up. Scott unclipped his safety harness and went below. At first his mind continued to buzz with unwanted thoughts. But, as the yacht rolled and yawed and the sea swished and hissed, he drifted away into sleep.

CHAPTER FOUR

The next thing Scott knew, he was being woken by daylight, shining in through the porthole the following morning. They were on the move. The boat bucked as she crested the waves. He looked out. They were heading south, away from the main islands. The sky was hazy, and already big clouds seemed to have built up out west.

Gina was still sleeping soundly. He didn't disturb her but went up on deck to get a better look at the weather. Ten o'clock and Gina was still zonked out. That *was* unusual.

Orlando was at the wheel.

'Where're we going?' Scott asked him.

'Hey! It walks! It talks!'

'I didn't sleep very well,' Scott mumbled.

Orlando laughed. He was glancing out west. Scott followed his gaze. 'A storm?'

'The weatherman says we *might* get lucky,' Orlando said, smiling and shaking his head slightly, clearly not believing a word of it.

'Tell me the bad news,' Scott said, worried. 'Will we get caught up in it or not?'

'Hey, man, my name ain't Nostradamus! Who knows?'

Scott kept on pushing for answers. 'Are we gonna head back to Roadtown now?'

'You should ask Mr Stone. He's the man.'

'It's OK, Orlando!' Clancy's voice cut across the discussion as he came up from below and joined them. 'You don't need to hide anything from Scott!'

Orlando nodded. 'Out here, you listen to the weather guys and you watch the screen, but you also get to *feel* the way it is. But right now, I ain't sure, and that's the truth.'

'Well,' Clancy said, 'the radio says we're way out on the edge of it.'

Orlando flicked a thumb towards the clouds. 'Yeah, but nobody tells those suckers which way to jump!'

'The sea is so rough!' Gina joined them from below, rubbing her eyes and looking less than pleased. 'I'm not going to get any photography done in this.'

'Wrong,' Clancy said, pointing south-east. 'That's where we're going, Three Parrot Island! There's a scuba trail along the reef. It's more sheltered beyond the island than it is here. You'll get your photos, don't worry.'

Scott glanced up ahead at a narrow island that was approaching fast. They were sailing on a long reach, forty-five degrees to the wind. A few boats were dotted about the island's green bays. The whole place was only a kilometre long by a hundred metres wide and it was shaped like a crescent.

One of the larger boats anchored offshore looked familiar to Scott. It was a great white sea yacht – the *Swordfish*. Yes! Cy!

Suddenly, the *Carolina* righted herself as Scott felt the wind change direction and the wind went out of her sails. He knew they would have to go off course to catch the wind again and he looked towards Clancy and Orlando to see what they would do.

'We'll have to use the engine,' Clancy said, starting it up.

Although the engine kicked in, Scott could hear it straining. Orlando gave it more throttle, but it didn't sound right.

'What's up?' Scott asked.

'Not sure,' Clancy replied, frowning.

Orlando went below decks, leaving Clancy at the wheel.

Moments later, Orlando called up. 'Can't see anything obvious, Clancy.'

Clancy wasn't the kind of person to be thrown by glitches like this, but Scott noticed his grimace of annoyance.

However, they managed to cruise slowly on to a good spot in the bay, then they anchored up.

Clancy sat scowling at the instruments in the cockpit in frustration. 'What do *you* reckon, Orlando? The boat got all checked out – got its certificate of safety. Sam said nothing about problems.'

'There was a bit of trouble with the winches when we hit rough weather, that's all,' Orlando said. 'But it was A–OK after that. You know me. I wouldn't be here if there was anything wrong.'

'Sure,' Clancy said, looking thoughtful. 'I know.'

'Is everything all right, Clancy?' Scott asked.

'That's what I'm checking,' he replied tensely.

Clancy tried the radar. Then he tried the

depth-sounder, the winches and the radio. 'Seems OK.' He looked puzzled.

Scott looked at his uncle staring at the dials, his hand on his chin and shaking his head slightly. 'Everything seems to be operating fine,' he said eventually.

Scott was about to ask whether they should turn back when a loud noise made them all look down over the side of the boat.

A red Kawasaki jet ski came zooming up and Cy grinned up at them. 'Hi, you guys. We saw you arrive. You wanna have a go on one of these? We've got two more.'

Scott looked at Gina lying on the deck.

'No thanks!' she said, pointing to her camera, which was ready for her dive. 'I want to get some shots of the reef.'

Clancy nodded to Scott. 'You go. Me and Orlando have got some more checks to run.'

Cy gave Scott a ride and, in no time at all, as the wind whistled through his hair, any worries about the *Carolina* had drifted away. Scott decided that, come what may, he *would* have a good time.

'Hey! What's that?' Scott shouted over the howling engine. He was pointing to a line of fluorescent buoys bobbing near a reef.

'Scuba trail. Fancy it?' Cy yelled. 'That's where your sis is probably headed.'

'That's Gina's thing. We both learned down on the Florida Keys, but I'm not very good at it – got no eye for it. She's the expert – the one with webbed feet!'

They both laughed.

Soon they were alongside the *Swordfish* where a second jet ski was ready for action – a white machine with a yellow flash.

A man with a mass of curly blond hair peered over the side of the yacht.

'Just going for a ride with my friend here, Dad,' Cy told the man.

Cy's father smiled. 'Sure, have a good time – but watch the weather.'

Scott eased on to the white-and-yellow craft.

'Are you OK with these?' Cy asked.

'Yeah. Never owned one, but rode plenty. This is a nice Sea-Doo GSX but that …' his eyes ran over Cy's red monster '… is something else! You lucky dog, an Ultra 150!'

'Fancy a race then?' Cy asked, grinning.

'Oh, yeah, that monster you're sitting on will do …'

'Zero to sixty in five seconds!' Cy said, bobbing alongside. 'You try it, but take it easy – the sea's picking up a bit!'

Scott felt great to be trusted with a fast racer by a boy he hardly knew. In ten minutes, they were flying about the bay, way beyond the reef. There were no divers' buoys out there so it was safe to have fun.

Even at less than maximum speed, their jet skis leapt like broncos off the crests of the waves. And there were no swimmers to look out for here. Two boats had raised anchor and sailed away since the *Carolina* had arrived.

As they roared past Clancy's vessel, laughing and shouting, they saw a diving buoy close in to the reef. That would be Gina with her camera.

Now the boys turned towards the open sea, running once more into the larger waves out there. Cy led the way and Scott powered alongside.

'First one to the island,' Cy said, pointing to a small piece of land about a kilometre away.

Scott laughed as Cy blasted away. Catching him would be easy. But then he saw the speed of Cy's craft. He had miscalculated. Time to open up. For ten seconds he accelerated, bumping and bopping his way across the crests of waves, but when he arrived he found Cy already there – grinning.

Scott laughed. 'This is just great!' He glanced back to the other island.

They kept their machines idling in the shallows and looked around for some new point to race to. As Scott grew used to the sound of the engines, he could hear something bleeping on Cy's jet ski. There was a waterproof box to carry things. The boy fished out a short-range radio: it was his dad. 'Really?' he said. 'No kidding? OK, will do!'

'Problems?'

'Yes,' Cy said. 'The front's changed direction, it's heading this way. If it really starts blowing, you don't wanna get caught out here in the open.'

Within seconds they were on their way back. Scott felt a twinge of regret that their fun had been cut short, but Cy was right: there was no shelter here, no protection.

Cy's dad was waiting on the deck of the *Swordfish*, looking a bit edgy.

'When are we leaving, Dad?' Cy had obviously got the message.

'Right now!' his father replied. 'This could be a bad one, it's building up fast. We're gonna head back to Roadtown just in case things get really rough.'

'Don't you know for sure?' Scott asked anxiously.

'Nobody knows, that's the problem. These storms go where they like. Sometimes they hit colder air and kind of bounce off like a racket ball.'

'How fast do they move?' Scott's interest was increasing as the *Swordfish* was already rocking and bumping quite a bit.

'Depends. They can sometimes move around fifty or sixty miles in an hour. There are no rules, really. Storms do whatever they want to do!'

Scott began to feel very uneasy. The dark clouds on the horizon were nowhere near fifty miles away. 'I'd better get going, then,' he said. 'I guess we'll be heading back too.'

Cy rode him over on the back of his jet ski.

'Which way are you headed?' Cy said as he prepared to zoom away.

'We were planning to go along the outer rim.'

'You ever been out in a storm?' Cy asked.

'Not really,' Scott admitted. 'Not a big one.'

Cy smiled. 'It's fun – but not at the time! Afterwards, you tell everyone about it and laugh.' Then he smiled. 'Take care! It's been great meeting you! See you around!'

Cy was about to blast off when he turned again. 'And be careful!' he said. Then he revved up and was gone in a spray of foam.

The powerful engine of the *Swordfish* had already been revving up while Scott was on its deck. Within a minute of Cy arriving back on board, it thundered off in the direction of Tortola.

The *Carolina* was not yet under power and Clancy was looking a bit concerned. Gina was back on board, packing her diving equipment away in a storage hole.

'I'm still not very happy with the boat, but it'll do the job,' Clancy said. 'We'll only lose a day or so by checking it out in a main harbour. We can't stick around here in a storm.'

Scott was still looking at the towering clouds in the distance. 'Cy's dad says that the storm could be a big one. They're heading back to Tortola.'

'Yeah, they're using their engine *and* sail. We can't take the chance of getting caught by it halfway back.' Clancy said nothing about their unreliable engine right then. He didn't need to. The thought loomed large in Scott's mind, and he saw the concern in Gina's eyes.

Clancy stood casually by Orlando, as the latter took the wheel. 'When I catch up with

Sam, I'm going to ask him some tough questions. Hit it, Orlando!' he said. 'Let's go.'

The engine boomed into life and Scott felt relieved. At least they were *doing* something, not just hanging around at the island like sitting ducks.

CHAPTER FIVE

Clancy fiddled with the weather radar on the *Carolina* as Scott and Gina looked over his shoulder.

'How does it look, Clancy?' Gina asked.

'Windy! Let's go below and I'll show you what we're going to do,' he replied.

When they got down there, Clancy unrolled a chart. 'We'll head out wide towards Antigua and get clear of the reefs.'

Scott stared at the chart and saw that there was a whole chain of islands all the way from the Florida Keys down to Trinidad. First the Bahamas, then the stretch of clear ocean they were supposed to be crossing, then the Virgin Islands where they had started, finally the Leeward and Windward Islands.

'See here,' Clancy began. 'There are a lot of islands, but also a lot of open water. With a storm blowing hard from the south-west, a boat could be pushed to the east and through the gaps. We are right on this last line of islands.'

'What's further out than this?' Gina wanted to know.

'Africa!' Scott said. 'Three thousand miles east.'

The problem they faced was obvious from the chart in front of them.

'You can anchor up and try to ride it out,' Clancy said, 'or get clear so that you aren't smashed up on any islands or reefs.'

'But Cy's dad has headed for Tortola,' Scott said.

'Sure. They're using the increasing wind to get them there fast. *And* they're sure of their engine.' Clancy pointed to a space between islands on the chart. 'If we get caught without power, we might end up *here* in the worst of the weather. *That* is the last place we want to be.' He pointed again. 'But *here*, to the south-east, we're closer to shelter, there's a whole string of islands and we'd be going away from the weather. That's the way for *us* to go. Less risky.'

Suddenly Clancy was out of the cabin and on the radio again.

Scott looked at the chart, then he looked at Orlando. The big man caught his gaze and nodded silently, indicating his agreement with the skipper's decision.

'Good, good!' Scott heard his uncle saying up above.

When Clancy ducked back into the cabin, he was smiling. 'Antigua say it's OK down there right now. So, the sooner we head there, the better!' He rolled up the charts. 'You two had better eat lunch while you can. We've already had ours.' He disappeared up to the cockpit to take the helm.

Orlando sorted out some Jamaican chicken wraps in the galley and dropped them on to the cabin table before going to join Clancy.

Beyond the shelter of the little island, the boat soon began to rock and roll as the waves grew bigger. Gina and Scott ate their meal as fast as they could and tried to think positively about their situation.

'We'll be OK, Gina,' Scott said as he tucked some of his possessions into drawers and cupboards. 'Clancy has got a plan to get us out of this bad weather.'

Gina laughed nervously. 'I know. He's great, isn't he?'

Minutes later, Orlando and Clancy came below to put their life-jackets on.

'You two need to get yours on too,' Clancy said. 'That inshore gear won't do in this weather.'

When Clancy had gone, Scott and Gina unbuckled their SOS life-supports, a kind of inflatable bum-bag. Now they put on the foul-weather jackets which were orange, waist length and sturdier, with a whistle, a light and a big, solid-metal ring for clipping lines to. *These* were life-jackets to keep you alive in the water. *Maximum protection.*

Gina peered through one of the portholes in the saloon at the scene outside. 'It's raining, Scott.'

Scott joined her and looked through the same hole. 'And the waves are really kicking up now.' Suddenly the yacht lurched violently, causing him to bang his head on the wood panelling. 'Ow!' he cried.

'You OK?'

'I'll live!' he said, rubbing the sore spot on his forehead.

Beyond the window, a great black wall of

cloud was heading their way from the south-west.

Scott's mind was racing. He'd sailed quite a few three- and four-metre dinghies in fine weather off Cape Cod, but he'd never faced anything like this. What made his anxiety worse was the fact that he'd recently read a book called *The Perfect Storm*. It was about trawlers ten times the size of the *Carolina* going down under thirty-metre waves. He knew what the sea could do. When he'd been laughing with Cy, the storm had just seemed another adventure on water, like his white-water canoeing trip. But on the canoeing course you knew where the danger started and where it stopped. You knew that in a few minutes you would be past all the savage rocks and cruel currents. Even if you flipped and got trapped underneath, there were safety boats to get you clear. Here, it was just the four of them, the *Carolina* and the sea.

Scott needed to think about something else. He tried to get Gina to talk about what she'd seen on the reef that afternoon. She told him about all the multicoloured varieties of fish she'd seen. Unfortunately, the storm warning had cut her photo session short and she had taken only eleven shots. Scott told her about the jet ski race. But they just couldn't concentrate, and soon the conversation dried up.

Moving with the boat as it rocked about was a bit like snowboarding, all knee-bends and balance.

'I wonder how rough it can get?' Gina wondered.

Even as she said it, the boat took a big hit from a wave, sending Gina crashing to her knees. As Scott rushed to help her he was hurled backwards into the bookshelves and fell to the floor himself. 'This is rough,' he muttered, rubbing his back.

'Hmm,' she said as they both struggled to their feet.

As they clutched the table, the boat took another big hit. It pitched and rolled violently at the same time. Scott was starting to feel sick. He was convinced that his face was turning a lurid shade of green. Gina, however, must have been born with sea legs. She never got sick, not on rollercoasters, not ever. Searching through his kit, Scott finally found the seasickness pill he was looking for. He swallowed it down thankfully.

'*Could* we sink?' Gina asked urgently.

'No way,' Scott said. 'These boats are built

to take it.' He only wished he felt as sure as he sounded.

Over the next few hours and into the afternoon, blackness ate up the whole sky. The great storm came racing towards them, stacking up waves that hurled the *Carolina* around like a dinghy. There were flashes of lightning. Huge, dark lines of intense rain ran like a curtain of bullets ahead of the swirling seas. Scott and Gina just hung on and tried to control their fears by talking down the risks and making plans for Antigua. Scott even fished out a scuba guidebook and struggled to discuss the best underwater trails.

Then the saloon door flew open and white spray poured in. Orlando poked his head into the calm.

'What a ride! Any chance of a drink up here, guys? Soon there won't be time for one!' he yelled and was gone.

'OK, no problem!' Scott yelled over the roar of the waves. He stepped cautiously into the galley. He poured some cold drinks into spill-proof bottles and edged past Gina towards the hatch. He took a deep breath and slid it back.

An icy sheet of salty spray lashed him in the face and stung his eyes.

Scott turned his face away, but it was too late. The water had already soaked his face and hair and dribbled down his neck.

He cursed and edged outside and up the steps. At the top he quickly clipped a safety line on to himself. He suspected he might need it.

The scene outside had been fearsome when seen through the cabin porthole. In reality it was far worse. Water lapped across the deck. The sky looked thunderous and rain pelted down all around – a relentless patter adding to the crack of breaking waves and rolling sea.

The *Carolina* suddenly lurched again and sent Scott jerking clumsily back down the steps. He cannoned into the saloon door. Hunching, he took the hit with his left shoulder. He steadied himself, but then thudded into the woodwork again as the boat pitched once more.

'You OK?' Orlando shouted over the wind at the top of the steps. Scott nodded and made his way back up again, grabbed a rail and handed the drinks to Orlando.

Scott focused on Clancy at the helm, holding the wheel steady.

'Thanks – you'd better get back down below straight away!' Orlando shouted above the noise. 'It ain't no picnic up here.'

Scott turned to go, but, above the howling wind that was singing in the rigging, came the sudden tearing sound of shredding sail – one of them was loose!

Clancy swore.

Another wave slapped Scott to the floor by the saloon door. He fumbled around blindly, trying to unhook his safety line. He could not, dared not, open his stinging eyes.

Just as he managed to get the line away, the door-handle lunged open and Gina snatched at him, pulling him inside. The pitching of the boat made them roll over together towards the middle of the saloon.

Gina untangled herself first and rushed back to slam the door shut.

Momentarily unable to cling to anything solid, Scott rolled around like a pinball on the slippery saloon floor. His knee hit the side bench and his head cracked against a table leg before Gina was able to check his movement. He began to shake with fear and pain.

'Scott! Scott! Are you hurt?'

'Yeah … uh … yeah … ow!' he yelled, taking a further crack on the arm before grabbing the table leg. 'And my eyes are killing me!'

There was a big boom of thunder.

Inside the cabin was dim; outside, lightning flashes lit the sky. The *Carolina* was being tossed about like driftwood by the whirling, swirling sea.

Suddenly the boat swung side-on to the waves and the whole vessel went over at a sharp angle yet again. Gina snatched at the table and jammed her knees under it. Scott grabbed on to her midriff.

'We aren't going to make it, are we?' she gasped.

Scott's face was hard and tense. 'Yes, we are!' His voice was shaking, his body trembling from the beating he'd just taken from the sea.

Suddenly there was a blinding flash and the cabin lights went out. 'Oh no!' Gina gasped.

Scott could barely see her now, but he caught the unmistakable sound of fear in her voice.

Gina shouted out. 'We're sinking, we're sinking!'

'No!' Scott yelled as they hung on to each other. 'This boat is self-righting! Clancy knows what he's doing! Come on! Don't let's lose it!'

Despite his rallying cry, his body was shuddering with ripples of cold fear.

Scott's heart pounded. He looked into the abyss outside. Are we sinking? he thought.

CHAPTER SIX

Scott braced himself, ready to stand up, but Gina's cry stopped him. 'Look, Scott. There's a line over the side!' She was pointing to the nearest porthole.

A thin line hung, taut, in front of them.

Either Orlando or Clancy must be on the other end of it.

Scott's heart missed a beat, but there was no time to dwell on his fear; he had to do something. 'I've got to get up there!' he said, scrambling wildly along the edge of the table to lunge at the door-handle. Then he forced himself out on deck to face the fierce sea.

The wind was still blasting spray over the top, and the rain was heavier than ever. Scott clipped himself on to a safety line, then he looked up, afraid of what he might see. Above him, Clancy was slumped at the helm. Blood streaked the man's face. The wheel was spinning wildly. A safety wire hung, taut as a hangman's rope, over the safety rails on the port side. Orlando must still be attached.

The boat was out of control and taking a terrific hammering. At this rate she might well broach, turn turtle, Scott thought. She *should* right herself, but would she? The idea of three of them dangling in the water under the boat, with Gina trapped in the saloon, horrified Scott. He banged on the saloon door.

He had to think fast.

He needed help.

'Gina! Gina! I need you up here, quick!'

Scott positioned himself behind Clancy, then quickly unclipped his unconscious uncle from the helmsman's chair and let him slide down against him. Gina came up behind her brother and tried to steady him – he needed both hands to manoeuvre the injured man out of the cockpit and towards the saloon door.

Scott dragged Clancy across the deck towards the steps.

Before they could pull him all the way into the saloon, the boat took another big hit and keeled over dangerously. Water poured over the deck and in through the saloon door. Gina screamed as both Clancy and Scott toppled over and pinned her down. Then, as the boat righted herself, the weight lifted and both Scott and Gina managed to push Clancy through the water into the saloon, unclip his safety line and slam the door behind them.

The three of them were like drowned rats. Water swished about the saloon floor. Gina knelt next to Clancy and felt his pulse. 'He's still alive!' she said. Blood was running from their uncle's forehead and his face was grey. They hauled him through to a bunk. Gina went for the first-aid box by the saloon door while Scott secured the unconscious Clancy into a bunk as quickly as he could.

Gina clung to a leg of the bunk with one hand and mopped the blood off Clancy's forehead with the other.

As the boat twisted, taking another big hit, there was a loud thumping noise against the hull.

'Orlando!' Scott shouted. 'I've got to get up there and *do* something, get everything … under control. We can't just leave him. The auto-steer must be off. We're out of control.' He felt bruised, battered and very sick, but he knew that now was not the time just to sit back and let fate take its course.

Lurching to his feet, he made for the door.

'Scott!' Gina cried out, as he fought his way out. 'Be careful ... please!'

'I will!' he called back, and then he was gone.

It seemed to take Scott for ever to get back up to the cockpit. There were so many things to do. Should he attempt to control the boat or try to get Orlando back? He decided to take control of the boat first, rather than take the risk of joining the other crewman over the side.

He remembered seeing some rope in a cockpit seat locker, so he fished a long coil out to lash down the wheel to stop it spinning. He waited until the wheel was right at the end of a spin then he grabbed it and, as firmly as he could, secured it to a safety rail with the rope. Then he slid up into the helmsman's seat and fastened himself into the harness.

Scott looked about him and froze for a second. The world was a mad whirl of black sky, white foam and spray, spinning, twisting and leaping before his eyes. Lightning still flashed. The sails were tattered and the auto-steer vane on the mast was gone! No vane, no auto-steer! *And* all the lights on the instrument panel were dead! What else can go wrong? he thought desperately.

Scott looked across at Orlando's line. It was still taut. Would he be able to haul Orlando in? With the electrics dead, the main winches were useless. He'd have to try to winch him in by hand. He'd need Gina's help, but she couldn't care for Clancy *and* work a winch. She would have to help at some point. How long could Orlando wait? How long would Clancy's first-aid take? The dilemma gave Scott a splitting headache. He had to think straight. He had to prioritize. First – check out Orlando's condition.

Now the boat was on a steadier course but was still bucking threateningly from time to time as she took on the biggest swell he had ever experienced in his life.

Scott eased out of the helmsman's harness and clipped his safety wire to the port rail. Then he edged carefully forward to assess Orlando's position over the side. At this point the really big crests were coming about every ten waves. Scott moved with great caution.

There was a slight lull. Scott peered over the safety rail. Orlando was dangling limply from his line, waist-deep in the water, below the cabin window. About twenty minutes had passed since the first lightning strike. Scott couldn't get close. Orlando's arms were trailing below him. Scott wasn't sure whether the man was alive or not. He didn't dare lean over any further to find out – he didn't want to join Orlando in the water.

He really needed Gina's help. She must have tended to Clancy's wounds by now. In any case, if his injuries were really serious, they would not be able to do much more to help.

One of them would have to attach a line to Orlando while the other one operated the winch. It might be best if he did the winching and Gina did the fastening; he was the stronger of the two.

Suddenly the decision was taken out of his hands. Another big wave hit the boat, twisting her side-on to the crests. Scott grabbed his safety line, but he couldn't help but tumble, head first, over the rail and on to Orlando. Now Scott was stuck beyond the edge of the deck, with his legs dangling over the water.

Terrible feelings of panic and desperation ran through him.

He kicked rhymically against the side of the yacht to attract Gina's attention. Spray blasted him. On the next few big hits he went chest-deep below the surface.

Scott's strength was ebbing. He tried to pull himself up on to the deck, but his shaking hands slipped off the wet line. He made another massive effort, gained a fraction and fell back. He kicked the side again. 'Gina! Gina! Help me! *Help me!*' he yelled into the wind. Then he slumped down over Orlando.

He was feeling numb with cold and tiredness.

The sea was winning.

'Scott, Scott, what's happened?'

Gina appeared above him.

'Tried to check him out … slid off myself!' he yelled over the roaring waves. 'Help me back up – please!'

I don't want to go down there into the sea, he thought wildly. I don't want to die. Orlando's probably dead anyway. If my line snaps … Scott was almost at his limit.

'What shall I do?' Gina yelled, hanging on tight up above him.

'Fix a heavy line to the hand winch! Get the clip to me.'

A moment or two passed and then she came slithering along inside the safety rails and flipped the line to him.

'Is that strong enough?' she called anxiously.

'Yes!' he shouted back. But, in truth, he didn't know. He might end up strangling himself or getting swept away with Orlando if the line snapped.

Scott looked down at the hissing, fizzing foam of the sea around Orlando. Holding his own line, he swung his feet up to hook his toes on the edge of the rail. Relief flooded through him. Then he tipped upside down to dangle above the cold sea and Orlando. The water rushed at him as he hung there; it smashed into his face as he reached the injured man. His safety line was as tight as a guitar string. It creaked and stretched.

Scott, hanging far over, managed to clip the spare line on to the metal ring on Orlando's life-jacket – then *pow*! He was under the waves as the boat rolled downwards. Black water rushed over Scott's head. This is it! he thought. The line's broken! I'm gone!

But then the inky blackness went and he found himself, gasping and spluttering, face to face with Orlando. His nose touched the crewman's cheek, which was ice cold – but Orlando's eyes opened at the touch. He was still alive!

Then the boat righted herself. All the wires were still in place.

'Hang on!' Scott yelled. 'Hang on!'

'Ready?' Gina's voice came through the swish of the waves and the blast of the wind.

'Wind it!' he yelled. 'Steadily!' Scott's heart was thundering as white water from a breaking wave churned just below him.

Scott clung on with one arm on his line and the other on Orlando's as they inched their way upwards. Then Scott managed to straddle the safety rail, all the while trying to haul Orlando up. Fractionally, the big man was moving – but it was almost all down to Gina. Finally Scott was able to roll over the top of the rail. However, when Orlando got to the same height as the rail, he stuck – the line pinning his bulky life-jacket beyond it.

'I can't move him any further!' Gina called.

Scott tried to lift the life-jacket over the rail, but his arms were like jelly. Then he lay back, put both his feet against Orlando's body and pushed the man out and clear. Suddenly, Orlando flipped on to the deck like a great, long, orange eel as Scott slithered back with him.

Scott slumped back and closed his eyes. Water lashed the deck, he couldn't feel his fingers and he was dead beat, but at least Orlando was back on board. Scott crawled along the rail, taking care not to make any mistakes now that the rescue was almost complete.

Even though the deck was smooth and slippery and Gina was strong, it was still tough going, hauling Orlando along with them. He was tall and heavy but, with Scott's help, Gina managed to tip the injured crewman down the cockpit steps and, finally, slid him into the saloon.

'Is he conscious?' Scott asked, barely able to speak as he slammed the saloon door and temporarily cut themselves off from the ravages of the sea.

Gina checked Orlando's neck pulse. 'No, he's burned and cold and is suffering from shock. We'll have to use a survival bag and warm him up slowly.' She looked across at her brother. 'You were great, Scott, really great!'

'No,' he said, '*you* were great. You saved both our lives.'

The two of them shook with the after-effects of the tension and adrenalin.

'I never thought we'd do it. I thought the line would snap!' Gina sobbed as she tugged Orlando into a more comfortable position.

'Me too,' Scott mumbled as they struggled on.

'Help me get Orlando into his cabin,' Gina said.

They began to haul him, little by little, through the slippery saloon as it tilted madly, first one way, then another. 'You get all his wet gear off and get him into a warm sleeping bag. I'll check out Clancy,' she added.

Scott's arms were like rubber. It seemed to take ages to get Orlando sorted out.

Suddenly, after a period of relative calm, the boat began to judder and shake, twist and turn once more.

'Gina, we're out of control! I'll have to leave them both with you. I've got to get back up there!'

Gina seized his arms. 'Why? What can you do?'

Scott shrugged off her grip. 'Nothing! Something! Anything! I have to try to get us back on course.' He staggered to his feet, feeling nothing but a numb weariness. His legs were leaden and his clothes heavy and saturated with sea water.

He tottered up the cabin like a drunk. Gina called from the door of Clancy's cabin. 'He's come round! Clancy's come round!'

'Great but … got to … get up there.'

Come on! You've got to hang on, he thought. Got to! Come on, Scott!

CHAPTER SEVEN

Scott struggled back into the *Carolina*'s cockpit, to face his worst nightmare.

The boat twisted, pitched and rolled like a ride at a fun fair. At first, he was frozen to the spot, afraid of making his move for the helmsman's chair at the wrong moment. He knew that he had no margin for error.

The wheel was spinning wildly again. The loose rope attached to it whipped round uselessly. Scott paused. Tiredness was making him indecisive. He'd been a lot bolder the first time he'd gone up on deck. Once again he thought about dangling above the fast-running sea. He thought about the line snapping and being hurled into ten-metre waves to die on his own.

Just then, there was a momentary lull in the waves. He took three quick steps and snatched at the helmsman's harness, whipped it across him and clipped himself in.

Once he was secure, he felt a bit better. He had the curious sensation that he was in one of those funfair simulators when you fly a jet or plunge over Niagara Falls. He was in a disaster movie. The yacht was being kicked around by mountainous waves. He was just so worn out, physically and mentally, that, for a second or two, he made no attempt to control the spinning wheel. This isn't how you die, he thought, fifteen years old, skippering a big yacht in a storm. *No way!*

He timed his snatch at the wheel. *Yes!* The feeling of control felt good, even if it was an illusion and in reality the sea and the wind were winning.

Scott peered through the windscreen in front of him to see what was up ahead. Everything was a nightmare of white water and black sky, with the waves cutting mad angles across the horizon. Scott tried to change the boat's angle of attack, tried to cut diagonally across the waves, the way he'd been taught.

The yacht tilted desperately. The two men downstairs knew what to do, Scott thought.

But how long would it be before Clancy or Orlando had recovered enough to give him some advice? He peered at the controls, then flicked a few switches: nothing. He grabbed the mike that you could use to communicate with people below deck and clicked it: nothing. All the electrics were dead – he was in a desperate plight.

To get advice, he'd have to lash the wheel again, unclip his harness and make the dangerous journey through the incessant waves and spray down the steps to the saloon door. There was no doubt that he did need advice. His brain said 'Go!' but his body said 'No!'

The boat was still leaping like a rodeo horse – but at least she was not jinking from side to side as she had been before, taking big hits side-on from the waves.

Suddenly a great wall of water came thundering over the side, ramming the yacht right over on her port side. For a second, the angle was so acute that it looked as though the sloop would roll right over. Icy fear ran through Scott as he gripped on to his seat for dear life. He thought of Gina and the others below. If we go over, they've got no chance down there. How long can we last in these conditions? he wondered.

To starboard, a dark shape was coming up. Close to it the sea was very white. Was it rocks?

Scott hauled the wheel to the left. He looked down at the engine switch. Might as well give it a go anyway. Nothing. Again nothing. The black shape grew closer. Again.

Crunch!

The boat took a huge hit from something solid. Rocks! Terror locked Scott rigid. Could the boat take it? He thought that *he* couldn't take much more, but he had to.

Gina's voice came up from the saloon door through the roaring noise of surf, 'Clancy is asking, have you made a Mayday call on the radio?'

'Everything's dead! How is he?' Scott shouted.

'He's delirious!' she yelled back.

'And Orlando?' Scott's voice cracked with desperation.

'Still groaning. He's got burns. We've got to get him to a hospital.'

Clancy's face appeared at the saloon door. He was leaning on Gina.

'I should … I … I,' he said. Then he collapsed.

'Clancy!' Scott shouted. 'Gina! He mustn't come out here!'

The sight of Clancy chilled Scott to the bone. Now he felt even more responsible for them all. I haven't got to let this blow me away, he thought. I've got to stay in control.

Think! *Think!*

Can we make land? He looked around. Rocks and reefs usually had islands near them, but as he scanned the dark horizon he saw nothing in the swirl of clouds and rain.

Scott tried the radio. He flipped a reserve switch and this time, somehow, a faint light came on. Was there emergency battery power? He turned to Channel 16, the standard emergency channel, and repeated 'Mayday! Mayday! Mayday!', the international distress call, over and over again. He couldn't remember the proper sequence of call signs – but it didn't matter anyway. The light on the switch dimmed and went out. Even if a message was possible, the lightning would have damaged the aerial as well as the auto-steer when it hit the mast. No aerial, no message.

Then he thought of something else. They had an emergency beacon, a sort of canister that sent out radio signals to coastguards. The chance it offered energized him enough to lash up the wheel again.

He slipped off the helmsman's harness,

clipped on a safety line to the back rail and carefully hauled himself across to the cockpit locker where the beacon was stowed. As soon as he left the security of the chair, Scott got an unpleasant surprise. While he had been at the wheel he had felt secure, but now, held by just a slim line, he started to feel nervous again. There was tension in his movements now because everything he did was too important. The deck was slippery and constantly changing angle. His fall over the side had sapped his confidence.

Scott found the canister, glanced at the instructions, then got ready to tie the beacon on to the stern of the ship. Slowly he eased his way along the rear guard-rail with it in his hand. Shall I tie it up first, then pull the string to activate it? Or shall I start it first, he thought.

He decided to loop the rope around a guard-rail first. The sea had eased a little, just what he had been hoping for. He took the ropes to secure the device but, just as he did this, the first huge wave for a while sent the boat leaping upwards and backwards. Scott crashed over the guard-rail and made a despairing grab for it. The precious canister fell from his fingers on to the slippery rear deck and rolled slowly towards the dark sea.

He stood up, slipped, stood up again and lunged forward, but the safety line pulled tight on him as his wet fingers clutched at the beacon ... and it slithered, spinning down the stern steps, into the sea.

He could not tell whether it sank or floated. It didn't matter, because the transmitter string had not been pulled. The message would have alerted the coastguards to their plight at once. Scott beat his fist on the deck in anger and frustration. Then he lay still and stared at the point where it had disappeared, even though water was crashing all over him. For a moment or two, anguish and disappointment flattened him. He wondered whether he had just let all their lives slip through his fingers ...

CHAPTER EIGHT

Over the next few hours the wind calmed a little.

Scott stayed slumped in the helmsman's chair, almost too tired to think. At present they were drifting downwind. As the swell eased he tried to keep watch, but he was actually floating in and out of sleep. Sometimes he looked up at the stars. That's the drinking gourd, the Plough, that's the North Star – so we're running north now, moving away from the storm. Good news, Scott thought, but how far out to sea are we?

The sea was still quite rough, but the waves were no longer big enough to capsize them. The overcast sky was to the west now. The storm had turned north and was leaving them behind. There was no moon, the ocean was dark and there wasn't a boat in sight. We've got flares but there's nobody here to see them, Scott thought. His lips were very dry and he was just thinking of stirring himself enough to struggle below when the saloon door opened and, with perfect timing, Gina appeared with a drink.

'This is better!' she said, looking around her. Foam was no longer breaking on the deck.

Scott took the drink gratefully. 'Oh, great, thanks!' he said. 'How are they?' he added, realizing that in his zonked-out state he hadn't checked up on the rest of the crew for a while.

Gina looked more than a little concerned. 'On and off, Clancy's OK, but then he drops right off to sleep.'

'Concussion. Remember Ricky Andrade in that South Side High game, when he got that elbow in the face from their pivot? He was so confused he even thought he'd done his Spanish homework!'

'What more can we do?' Gina asked, ignoring his lighthearted remark.

'Just let him rest, I guess. I'm no medic. What about Orlando?'

'I think he could be really bad, Scott. Do you want to come and see?'

'OK,' he said. The sea had calmed down and he saw no present risk in going below. Scott eased himself stiffly out of his seat to go down the steps and into the saloon. Gina made a move to go below with him.

'Can you keep watch while I'm down there? I think we should have somebody up here. The flare gun's in there.' He pointed to a locker.

'OK,' she said.

Gina clipped herself into the helmsman's chair.

When he got below, Scott found Clancy lying in his bunk with his head down over a chart. The cabin was lit by a battery-powered lamp.

'Clancy? Clancy!'

Scott's uncle looked a mess, with his head swathed in a bloody bandage. The ordeal had put years on him. His eyes were bloodshot and slightly unfocused. His tanned face had lost its colour.

'Mayday …' Clancy murmured.

'We tried, Clancy, but … everything's dead.'

'Dead?' Clancy looked up, confused. Gina *must* have told him.

'Yes, Clancy, dead. We're drifting without power.'

'What about … the reserve? Ask Sam … to take a look.'

'That, too – and Sam's not here. He didn't come with us, Clancy.' Sam! thought Scott. Sheesh! We really *are* in a mess if Clancy is as bad as this!

'Drifting … you say … how long?'

'Er … three … hours.'

Clancy pointed to the chart. '… which means that we might be somewhere … somewhere …' and he sank slowly down until his head was resting on the chart.

Scott eased him gently back on to his pillow.

Scott felt the skin across his forehead tighten with tension. Clancy couldn't help right now. He too was obviously badly in need of hospital treatment.

Scott looked in on Orlando. The crewman was conscious and struggling to control his pain. However, his mind was clearer than Clancy's.

'Do you want a drink?' Scott asked him.

'So long as it ain't sea water!' Orlando gritted his teeth, trying to smile, but Scott could see that his hair was burned and he lay curled awkwardly as if the fall over the side had hurt his right arm and side.

Scott returned from the galley in a

moment, and Orlando nodded gratefully as he sipped the orange juice drink.

'You know,' Orlando said, 'we'll have to do this again some time!' Then he closed his eyes as pain twisted his face.

Scott smiled grimly at the joke, then eased his way back on deck.

Gina huddled like a winter sparrow at the helm.

'Anything?'

She shook her head.

'Get some rest,' he said, gazing about him and noting the improving weather. 'Looks like we're clear of the worst.' He smiled, and she kissed him on the cheek before disappearing wearily below deck.

Scott fixed his harness and sat at the wheel, thinking, We're way out east somewhere. They must have air and sea searches for people who are missing. But then he thought, We're not 'missing', we're just cruising, heading for Antigua.

The boat was magnificent to look at, wonderful. So, how could they get into a fix like this? All this radar and stuff — then whammo, a big strike, and there they were on nothing but a luxury raft!

He had a sudden thought. Maybe the

electrics are not beyond repair? If only Orlando and Clancy weren't hurt, maybe they could do something?

Then Scott thought about the water in the saloon. We might be leaking, but what can we do? he thought. If it was calm and daylight, Gina or I could swim under and have a look underwater but … It would be a long night.

By now Scott was almost past tiredness and his mind was drifting. He started thinking about his mom and gran, waiting up at Bimini. Dad was gone. The loss of Clancy, Scott *and* Gina would be too much for Mom to take. Then he flopped back. Will I ever see Mom again?

The sea was calmer now, but the unwanted thoughts kept coming back to him. Where are we? What's going to happen to us? He hated feeling helpless.

From time to time, he came upright with a jolt. He kept thinking that the sea ahead was foaming. But no, it was just his tired mind playing tricks. Now the swell was getting less and less. Yet still the sloop rode low. He slumped down in his chair and ate a banana that he'd found in the galley, though he was feeling almost too tired and sick even for that. He started to drift away into sleep as the

Carolina struggled on and the stars were the only lights on the great, dark sea.

CHAPTER NINE

Scott drifted in and out of sleep during the night.

He remembered time passing in little jumps, like broken bits of film stuck together. He thought he recalled flashbacks of a dark sea and a gradually brightening sky.

Scott woke, feeling as though he'd been kicked all over by a team of mules. His mouth tasted as though Long John Silver *and* his parrot had slept in it!

He jerked upright as their real-life dilemma came flooding back to him.

Back to work.

A glance at the compass showed him that they were now drifting west-north-west on the prevailing current, with the hazy morning sun behind them.

Was the storm over?

It appeared so, but nevertheless something felt wrong. The *Carolina* was … too low.

He looked over the side and saw that the waves lapping against the hull of the boat were far higher than they should have been. His brain froze. This didn't matter so much when the water was calm like it was now – but, if the storm returned, they would sink in no time at all.

Scott's stomach lurched with pangs of hunger. He moved gingerly towards the steps to go below, his legs like lead weights, drained of energy.

He looked up. All around, the horizon was empty.

He stopped in his tracks when, for the first time, he noticed up ahead a long line of foam that indicated a reef stretching right across their course.

They were drifting towards it, but they had no power to pull away from it. If they sank here, the *Carolina* would just vanish without trace.

The end of the storm had lulled him into a false sense of security. While he had rested, a new and equally threatening danger had crept up on them.

He raced below, an icy chill running up and down his spine.

The saloon was knee-deep in water now.

He hadn't realized that things were so bad.

'Gina!'

Scott's sister was lying asleep on the long seat against one wall. Sea water lapped against her makeshift bed – just below the level of her head.

She sat up, startled to be woken so abruptly. 'Quit it! What are you shouting for … Oh, no! We're sinking!'

'Not yet, we're not!' Scott sloshed through the water towards the cabins. 'Orlando! *Orlando!*'

On his bunk, the crewman's eyes flicked open. He moved his head slowly to face Scott and Gina, who were standing over him.

'Orlando,' Scott asked, 'have we got a manual bilge pump?'

Orlando shook his head. 'Those diddy things are no use on a boat like this!' He stared down at the water all around. 'You can't hand crank nine thousand gallons an hour. That's what it'd take to clear this boat.'

'Is there *no* back-up to the electric pumps?' Scott gasped.

'Yeah, but it's *mechanical*. Runs off the engine drive.'

The drive of the *dead* engine, Scott thought.

Just then a big, wet, filthy figure came looming up out of the after bilge area and Clancy slumped to the table. He looked ragged and wild. His bandage was black, bloody and oily. Scott was stunned by his appearance, amazed at his courage and determination. 'This leak … can't fix it! Can't find it! Got to get ready …'

'What can we do, Clancy?' Gina said desperately.

'I was sure we hit rock last night. Are we holed?' Scott asked.

'No, we'd be sinking even faster,' their bloodied uncle said. 'Can only think it's … maybe the prop shaft …'

'And?' Scott's voice wobbled.

'If you have a gap where the drive shaft exits the boat, it's … like a pipeline into the hull. Can't be such a big hole – but it's big enough.'

'We've got a reef ahead, too,' Scott told them.

'How far?' Clancy asked.

'Maybe fifteen minutes away, maybe longer. I'm not sure.'

Clancy's face crumpled.

The *Carolina* was doomed. It was less than two days since they had left port, but it felt like a month.

'Shall I launch the life-raft?' Gina shuffled about, looking agitated.

Clancy shook his head. 'Not yet. Let's get Orlando on deck first. Then we'll make sure we've got everything we need. No coming back ... Then maybe you can inflate the raft while Scott and me stow some survival gear in the dinghy. Gotta get these clothes off first.'

He didn't say it, but Clancy had just given his final order as skipper of the *Carolina*. They were preparing to abandon ship.

Scott snapped into action. He took Orlando by the body and Gina supported his legs. Orlando wrapped his good arm round Scott's neck and they paddled carefully through the water in the saloon and cautiously up the steps and laid him on the foredeck. The boat was still rocking – but now rhythmically, without the abrupt jolts of the day before.

As soon as Orlando had been made comfortable they all changed into dry clothes, busying themselves in silence. They packed their personal gear into their rucksacks and piled them up on the cockpit steps. Scott brought up the two yellow emergency-supply bags from a locker by the galley. Gina took the orange life-raft from its fitting by the aft rails, secured it firmly to the rails and flipped it over the side to self-inflate.

Scott checked for the little grey offshore inflatable dinghy with its tiny engine that he hoped was still bobbling behind the boat. It was still there, securely fastened to the *Carolina*. Relief poured through him. He knew it was going to be a big advantage in their forthcoming bid for survival when they left the main boat.

Clancy leaned heavily on a safety rail, his hand on his forehead. He still looked in great pain. 'Listen, guys,' he managed to say. 'We've got to decide now what to do.' He paused, dragged himself over to one of the cockpit locker seats and sank down. His earlier efforts below were obviously catching up with him. 'Maybe … we can get the dinghy heading west. The outboard's only for harbour work, really … but we've got to make a move.'

'Do we have to get off now?' Gina asked. 'We might not sink for ages.'

'Yes, but … see there?' Clancy pointed

towards the sea around them. Already the water was darker and the reef was only a few hundred metres away. While they had been working, the *Carolina* had drifted ever closer to the danger below the surface.

Gina stared ahead at the reef. 'Maybe we'll just float over it.'

'Maybe, but we're getting lower in the water every minute. We should prepare … for the worst,' Clancy replied.

Scott had a plan. 'Look, the inshore dinghy will fit the three of you, with Orlando lying down. I could take the life-raft. I'm sure I could last more than a week on an emergency pack. You'd be back for me within a day or two, surely?'

There might have been an argument but, just then, a faint drone came from far away to the north.

'A plane!' Scott was jumping about. 'Look, a plane! Hey!'

In a second Gina was next to him, waving madly. 'Hey! Hey! Over here!'

The plane was headed west, parallel to them. It did not change path, but they both shouted anyway.

Clancy held his head. 'Flares. Got to fire … flares!' He struggled to open a cockpit seat-locker, removing a flare gun and loading a red flare. He held the gun above his head and pointed it towards the distant plane.

Whap! The red flare rocketed into the sky.

Seconds later, he fired an orange smoke flare that billowed from its canister as it floated on the water.

The drone of the plane was very far away now.

'It's a seaplane,' Gina said, peering through binoculars. Then, after an age, she said in a low voice, 'It's not turning.'

Scott's face twisted with frustration. Their bodies were exhausted and their minds were tired but, most of all, their hearts were weary. After surviving all the bumps and near-disasters in the storm, they were rapidly running out of spirit. For the first time, in spite of himself, Scott thought they might not make it.

'There will be other planes,' Clancy said hopefully.

We've got to get going soon, Scott thought. Orlando won't get any better here. We can't have anything else going wrong. Those clouds aren't going to go away.

Clancy came up behind them, his face creased with tension. He put one big hand on each of them. 'You're … doing great, guys.'

His voice was very low and tired. He was rocking from side to side. He had made a big effort to pull things round, but now he looked exhausted.

Scott suddenly noticed that they had reached the reef.

A scraping noise made them all tense up.

The hull of the *Carolina* touched the reef for a few moments, the boat wobbled, then their momentum carried them free again.

Scott felt the tension building up inside him. He was itching to get going. The *Carolina* was finished, dream yacht or not.

'Clancy, we've got to *go* before we hit. We can't get Orlando off here in a hurry.' Scott remembered how awkward it had been to get Orlando back on the *Carolina* when he had gone overboard. 'And also,' he added, 'the seaplane wasn't very high, so maybe we're not that far away from one of the bigger islands.'

Gina looked from Clancy to Scott, and then back to Clancy. 'How about it, skipper?' she urged.

The five-second gap before his reply seemed to last for ever.

'Well, I guess …' Clancy's voice was slow again.

But those three words were enough.

Gina and Scott were already on their way to the foredeck. Fortunately, Orlando was able to hobble, with their support, slowly and obviously in great pain, down the after steps. Gina stepped first into the dinghy and eased him down. The graceful, athletic crewman now lay like a crippled spider, occupying a lot of space. Scott brought cushions from the saloon to make the man more comfortable. Orlando gave him a thankful grimace but did not speak.

As the *Carolina* scraped against the coral again, Scott quickened his pace.

'Right, Gina,' he said. 'You stay there and hang on to Orlando, and I'll get the gear.' He looked around.

Clancy was standing in the cockpit. His uncle didn't seem able to take his eyes off the dancing foam that marked the sharpest points of the reef which lay in wait for his lovely boat.

Scott brought the raft round to the dinghy and tied them together by securing a strong rope from a metal ring on the life-raft to a tethering point on the dinghy's bow. He threw a survival pack and the rucksacks into the life-raft. Then he handed another yellow survival pack and Orlando's and Clancy's gear to Gina.

The boat rocked again. This time the

crunching sound was louder. Surely the hull had suffered even more damage this time?

'Come on, Clancy,' Scott called out urgently. He glanced towards his sister. Gina was getting ready to untie the dinghy from the *Carolina*.

'We might just clear …' Clancy started saying, when *Crrunch!* – the reef bit into the hull and the *Carolina* was brought to an abrupt stop.

Clancy was hurled flat on to the slanting deck and Scott found himself clinging desperately to one of the safety rails.

'Clancy!' Scott shouted, scrabbling across the deck to help the big man up and back to the stern. His uncle's face was ashen and there were tears in his eyes as Scott dragged him over the edge and lowered him into the life-raft.

'Now, Gina!' he shouted. 'Release the rope!'

The sloop had keeled over to thirty degrees, but they were still tied on!

Gina's hands worked in a blur, and seconds later there was space between both craft and the sinking boat.

The *Carolina* tilted even more, but the rolling waves pushed them rapidly away from the stricken vessel. Scott slumped in relief against a tearful Clancy.

'You all right in there?' he heard Gina shout

across to him from the dinghy.

In the life-raft Scott stirred. 'Yeah … we're all right,' he gasped in reply.

Clancy lay back, his face a mask of sadness. 'I always dreamt of owning a boat like that,' he said. 'Ever since I was a kid I've thought about it. Used to watch them leaving Newport, sailing out there into the sunset …'

Scott touched his arm. There was a terrible sadness in his uncle's lined face. His battered head seemed to droop and his powerful shoulders were hunched.

He was about to try to reassure him when Gina shouted across to him.

'The *Carolina*, Scott. Look!'

Scott and his uncle both looked up. A couple of hundred metres away, Clancy's beautiful white boat was toppling gently over into the waves. The decks slipped below the surface, yet still the graceful hull held up and the tall mast glittered as it stood proud of the swirl of foam.

Scott looked at Gina and Gina looked at Scott as their eyes also filled with tears.

'Goodbye, princess … !' said Clancy in a soft, crushed voice.

CHAPTER TEN

The two tethered survival craft drifted away from the *Carolina*, now just a flash of white hull and a mast sticking up into the sky. She couldn't sink any further now, but she was well beyond habitation.

Scott finally tore his eyes away from the boat, just in time to see Orlando struggling to sit up in the dinghy in order to be sick – half over the side and into the sea but half inside the craft.

'We've got to get him to a hospital, Scott,' Gina gasped. 'I don't know what to do for him! Uncle Clancy, take a look at him!'

Scott helped Clancy haul himself up. Scott and Gina exchanged stares. Clancy's eyes were like glass marbles. Only a couple of days ago he'd looked like Superman to them. Now he was just a sick, middle-aged guy.

'Uncle Clancy, can you go across and look at Orlando in the dinghy?' Scott asked. 'He's really sick. Gina doesn't know what to do.'

'No, we stay together,' Clancy mumbled.

Scott suddenly felt very agitated. He looked across to where the injured crewman lay with his eyes closed. 'Orlando *needs* you, Uncle Clancy. You've got to go to him. You've done first aid. The *Carolina* has gone. You can't bring her back. We've got to get out of here now! Swap places with Gina and see what you can do for him. *Please?*'

Clancy shook his head stubbornly. 'No, we've *got* to stay together. I *promised* your mom I'd look after you.' Scott wasn't sure any more how rational his uncle's behaviour was now.

Gina propped Orlando up against the side of the dinghy in case he needed to be sick again. 'Scott!' she said urgently. '*Quickly.*'

Sure enough, Orlando's body shook, and he was sick again into the waves.

Clancy watched his friend in pain. 'Let me ... let me have a look at Orlando,' Clancy said falteringly, as if he had only just thought of the idea.

Scott breathed a sigh of relief. He helped

Clancy clamber precariously across the metre-wide gap between the two bobbing craft.

On the dinghy there was little room, and Gina struggled to find a space for herself out of the way of the two men.

Clancy knelt over his friend. 'Orlando? Orlando?'

There was no reply. Clancy gave Gina an anxious look. 'He's unconscious again!' he said and rubbed his forehead.

Gina gave up trying to stay out of the way at last, and she wriggled carefully over to the side of the dinghy. 'I'm coming over, Scott,' she said as she stood up and made to jump across.

Scott was ready to catch her – but an unexpected bobbling of the dinghy sent Gina toppling, head first, into the gap between the two craft.

'Gina!' Scott cried.

His sister was splashing about in the gap and she spat some salty water out at her brother. 'Yuk!' she panted. 'I'm such an idiot.'

'Are you OK?' Scott asked, leaning forward and helping to tug her roughly into the life-raft.

Gina started laughing. 'Yes! I suppose so. It's just my pride that's hurt.'

Scott, despite their grave situation, smiled

for the first time in twenty-four hours. 'And you're wet *again*, Gina!'

Gina rubbed one of her hands. 'I think I scraped my hand on some coral,' she said.

'Let me see,' Scott said. He examined the hand, but there was no serious damage visible. Gina's hand was red where she had just rubbed it and there may have been the beginnings of a bruise – but, importantly, the skin wasn't broken.

'I'll live,' Gina said.

Before Scott could reply there was a shout from the dinghy.

'The rope!' Clancy's urgent cry cut through Scott like a knife.

He lunged past Gina towards the side of the raft and saw that there was now a two-metre gap between the two craft.

'Oh, no!' Gina cried. 'Scott, we've come adrift!'

The rope that had tethered Scott and Gina to Orlando and Clancy in the dinghy drifted uselessly between them in the bobbing waves.

Within seconds, the eddies and the current generated by the reef spun the dinghy away from them.

Scott reached out to Clancy, his arm stretched to its limit.

Clancy did the same and their fingertips touched briefly as the craft moved towards each other again.

But Scott could not hold on.

The current split two ways round a section of reef and they were metres apart again.

This time they did not bounce closer. They twisted even further apart.

'Try the motor,' Gina shouted to her uncle.

Clancy started fiddling with the outboard motor, but it wouldn't kick in. Scott seized a paddle and started to work like mad to close the gap between the two craft which had quickly stretched to nearly ten metres.

Progress was hard because the life-raft was being pulled along by the eddies around the reef much faster than the heavier dinghy.

They got to within about three metres of each other. Then Scott stopped and held the paddle across to Clancy to bridge the gap. His arms and shoulders were burning with the effort to stop them drifting apart.

Clancy stopped trying to get the motor going and reached out once again to bridge the gap. However, his fingers barely touched the paddle. He got a brief grip on the narrow end, but his weakened fingers could exert little pressure on it.

'I'm losing it, Clancy!' Scott shouted. Little by little his fingers were slipping away. 'I can't hold on!' Gina was holding on to Scott's legs, struggling to keep him inside the life-raft.

Clancy made a two-handed lunge to seize the paddle but, instead of his action pulling the life-raft closer, it just stretched him like a human bridge over the stern of the dinghy. He was a big man and the weight of the outboard was also at the stern, so his boat rocked wildly and, as he struggled for balance, the paddle flew away.

The loss brought Scott to a halt.

Clancy lay crumpled at the stern of his boat. Then he struggled to activate the motor again as the current swept the two craft apart once more. 'Sorry, sorry … my fault!' he croaked.

'No, I tied the knot,' Scott shouted as the gap quickly widened to ten metres or more.

Still there was no engine sound.

'We're drifting north-west. Got to hit something soon!' Clancy shouted. 'Sorry about … all this!'

'Stop saying that,' Gina said. 'We've just had bad luck.'

Now they were flying away, clear of white surf. The dinghy was still bobbing in the turbulence.

Clancy looked shattered. All the things he wanted to say were written on his face.

'We'll be OK,' Scott called, although that wasn't what he felt. It was time to grow up quickly.

'Please be careful,' Gina shouted. She couldn't help but cry as she spoke. Scott saw the twitch of her lips, saw how tight and pale her face was now.

'… soon!' was all they could make out of the next time Clancy shouted across.

They waved. 'We'll be OK. Really!' Scott shouted.

Soon the gap was fifty metres, then, in no time at all, it stretched to a hundred metres, then probably to two hundred.

At first Scott peered across through a pair of binoculars he had brought in his rucksack. To start with, Clancy fiddled with the motor, then he sat, staring at it, with his face in his hands and, quite soon, he flopped down out of sight.

'What's he doing?' Gina asked anxiously.

'He's lying down,' Scott said. 'I think he's exhausted.'

Gina zipped up the canopy of the life-raft a little to give her some shade.

Suddenly Scott started shaking. He was *so* hungry. Time to open the emergency pack.

He quickly removed a plastic container full of water and two plastic cups.

'Let's go easy with this stuff,' Gina said as she opened a bag of dried fruit. Scott tried to imagine that he was eating a cheeseburger. An energy bar was a slice of pizza with pastrami.

'How far out *could* we be?' Gina asked.

'It's really hard to say. If we'd had sail up with that big sea behind us on the *Carolina*, we could be way, way out. After the mainsail went we were just drifting north-west mostly.'

'But if we're going …' Gina trailed off.

'West-north-west,' Scott finished the thought.

'… we could drift wide of Tórtola over that deep!' She looked him in the eye for reassurance.

'No, I don't reckon we're that far north, or that seaplane wouldn't be heading north-west,' said Scott.

Gina nodded and lay back.

I'd better be right, Scott thought.

After a while Gina dozed off, leaving Scott alone with his thoughts. He scanned the horizon with the binoculars. Clancy's dinghy was gone. The sun was getting high in the sky now. The storm may have passed – but the menace of a vast, empty sea was just as great.

CHAPTER ELEVEN

Scott lay back against the side of the life-raft.

He was uncomfortable, so he blew up an inflatable pillow and jammed it under his head. Gina looked comfortable in the shade of the canopy, leaning on the rucksacks and other bags, so he made no attempt to disturb her sleep.

He could feel the water under the raft, and the sensation triggered off a worrying train of thought. He poked the inflatable side-wall with his finger. Was it a bit soft? Could it be deflating? The events of the last twenty-four hours had eroded his confidence. When you get on a plane, it flies – right? When you get on a boat, it floats – yes? Wrong! *Should* fly. *Should* float. Life-rafts *should be* reliable. We are just a few centimetres above the water here. In the *Carolina* they had been a *metre* or two above the surface, but it hadn't done them any good. The sense of security had been false.

Scott tried to get a grip on his nerves. I've got to switch off for a while – got to stop my head buzzing. He took his Walkman out of his rucksack, slotted in a tape and lay back. Perhaps music can take my mind off all this. After their restless night and all the disappointment of the day so far, he was drained of strength and spirit.

He closed his eyes against the blaze of the sun's bright heat and fell asleep.

When Scott woke up, it was around mid-afternoon. The sea was still choppy in the south-east breeze. He scanned the south-western horizon, looking for trouble. Maybe it was a little dull over there, but nothing scary. The outside of the canopy was wet. A convectional shower hadn't even woken him.

Gina opened her eyes. 'How are we doing?'

'OK. So far so good with the weather.'

Gina sat in the sun. Scott sat back in the

shade and opened and gobbled down a tin of peaches.

'I wonder how Clancy is doing?' Gina asked.

'He's a hard nut …' Scott said, '… head like a rock. Played football at college.'

'I was thinking about Orlando, too …'

'They're tough guys, these island sailors,' Scott said, picking up his binoculars again. 'I wonder if … Hey! Look at this!' He handed the glasses to Gina. 'What's that *there*?' He pointed ahead.

'I don't know,' she said, 'but it's floating. Something red … and what's that shadow … could it be … an island to the west, way out on the horizon?'

For half an hour they watched the dot getting larger. Then Scott wasn't sure. Perhaps he was fooling himself? If you stare at anything long enough, it gets bigger in your mind.

'Is it moving?' Gina asked.

Scott shook his head. 'No. Looks like a boat anchored up,' he said, 'but I can't see any movement on board.'

It was a powerboat.

'Anything new?' he asked when she took the binoculars.

'Powerboat. There's still nothing moving,

though,' she said. 'If it's deserted, maybe we could use it? Maybe this is our prayers answered.'

'Most likely it's broken down. Maybe they got marooned in the storm too? We could just join them until they are rescued!' Scott's voice went up a tone.

'Suppose it's someone who doesn't want visitors?' Gina said in a serious voice. 'There's nobody to help us out here!'

The other boat was about five hundred metres ahead and about a hundred metres to their left. They had no paddle and the only way to reach it would be to swim across at the time when they had drifted closest.

In ten minutes or so, they'd pass it by. 'There are hundreds of powerboats around here,' Scott reasoned. 'They can't all belong to villains!'

'We're going to drift by,' Gina said. 'I'd better swim across with a line.'

'No,' Scott said. 'When we get there, someone will have to hang on before they can tie up, and I'm stronger than you.'

'It's no use being strong if you don't make it across,' she said sharply. 'I'm a better swimmer.'

'Suppose they *aren't* friendly, Gina. It has to be me.'

'Stop being sexist. They could shoot you

just as easily as they could shoot me – right?'

'No,' he said, as if that was an end to the discussion.

'Scott!' she shouted. 'I'm going to do this! Like it or not!'

Scott glared at his sister momentarily, then he snapped into action. He tied a line to the metal loop of her life-jacket, and a second later she plunged in.

There was about fifty metres to make up. As soon as she set off, Scott could see how much a life-jacket hampered her normally fluent stroke.

The red boat grew closer and closer. Gina seemed to be slowing in the water. Twenty metres now. Ten. Alongside. Five, she was passing it. An anchor chain hung down from the stern. She snatched at it. The line to Scott went tense. He was paying it out like mad to release the pressure. He saw Gina swing her legs up on to the stern, clamber up and peer into the cockpit. Suddenly a man in a bright-green shirt popped up in front of her.

CHAPTER TWELVE

Scott peered hard at the man on the speedboat.

Unfortunately the appearance of the stranger distracted him from his job of paying out the line.

'Argh!' Gina yelled as she was hauled backwards into the sea by the taut line.

Somehow she managed to get her right arm tangled in the rope and she struggled to disentangle herself. The current was pulling her steadily along under the water. Scott couldn't see properly what was happening in the frothy bubbles surrounding her. He didn't want to start hauling her in if it would make things worse.

'Help us!' Scott yelled. 'Help us, please!'

The man in green was joined by another in a flowery shirt, and they both stood, watching, motionless and stony-faced. Scott thought there would be the rumble of powerful engines within seconds, but the powerboat, far from cruising alongside, remained silent and at anchor. They're not going to do anything, he thought.

Somehow Gina righted herself and Scott pulled with all his might as she struggled back towards him. Once again he felt afraid.

When his sister was within a couple of metres of him he became concerned that she was running out of energy and wasn't going to make it. He leaned out, snatched at Gina's arm to help her over the edge of the life-raft and in, showering water in every direction.

He grabbed a towel, wrapped it round her and gave her a hug. 'You were *fantastic*!'

Her face was very close. She was trembling. And wet again.

'That man never said a word! Not a word,' she gasped. 'Are they still there?'

Scott took a quick glance over her shoulder. The red powerboat was over a hundred metres away now. The men stood like sentries, watching, waiting.

'Yes,' he replied, 'and they haven't moved!'

'He gave me the creeps, that guy,' she said. 'His eyes were so … dead.'

'We *must* be near land, Gina,' Scott said, rubbing her arms dry. 'If they were smugglers or whatever, they're not going to rendezvous in the middle of nowhere, are they?'

For over two hours they kept an eye on the powerboat. It didn't move. Scott was glad. The men looked like bad news.

The life-raft was quite big for two people, and the sea wasn't rough. Even so, Scott wasn't looking forward to nightfall. He searched all around the horizon. The thin line that Gina thought might be an island was now to the south-west and they were drifting past it towards the setting sun.

Scott flopped down and peeled an orange. He was still low, but he wanted to take their minds off their present predicament. 'We'll be OK. It's not the first scrape we've been in, is it?' he said, handing her a couple of juicy segments.

'Hey,' Gina said, 'what's with this "scrapes *we've* been in" stuff? Don't you mean "scrapes *you've* been in"?'

Scott smiled. 'Well, if you put it like that …!' There was no denying what she said.

'What about when you got stuck, up on Lookout Mountain with Eric Boldon? Holed up in a storm with just *one* tin of beans because you left your pack in Janine Chadwick's car.'

'Yeah, but we had lots of firewood.' Scott's defence was pathetic.

'And then there was that time when you were camp cook with Mike Morris. You put five kilos of oatmeal in two litres of water instead of the other way round, and we had to cut it into slices ...'

'OK, OK!' Scott grinned. 'But nobody's perfect. How come *you* blew up the hot water boiler last fall in Bear Park Forest ...?'

'*You* told me how to light it!'

'Ah, yes!' Scott mumbled. 'So I did.'

His face went red and they both grinned.

'You've been stranded before, haven't you?' she said. 'How long was it you were down Chilcot Cave?'

Scott didn't smile. He felt cold inside. 'Too long.'

Two years before, Scott had been trapped down an old silver mine with Joe Gonzalez. It had started as a laugh. He never told anyone how scared he had been. It was like a rabbit warren down there. They *just* got lucky and stayed alive.

Cats have nine lives, Scott thought. I've used up two or three already.

He picked up his pack, and a torch fell out; it had Clancy's name on it. It jolted him back to the present. He couldn't bear to think about the fate of the two men. He had to concentrate his efforts on himself and Gina now.

As the sky darkened, Gina zipped up the life-raft canopy and clicked on the overhead light. She fished a book out of her pack and passed the time reading.

Scott just propped himself up by the opening, half watching the sky, half daydreaming. Gradually the western sky was turning from yellow to orange to fiery red as the sun dipped lower and lower. He stared into the sunset blaze. The horizon looked uneven, but he wasn't sure. Eventually the sun was balanced on the edge of the world.

'Gina? Can you see a light up ahead?'

She sat up and stared out at the great sea.

Suddenly the sun was gone. There was just an afterglow.

'I thought I saw something, on the horizon – there,' Scott added.

Scott had a small hand-held compass in his bag. The object he *thought* he had spotted was due west. They seemed to be drifting past it on the prevailing current. That is, if it *was* land.

He peered again. 'I just … can't … see … for sure.'

'It's OK,' she said, disappointed. 'Probably wasn't anything anyway.'

His eyelids were heavy. 'I'll keep watch,' he said.

Gina nodded and returned to her book. However, in no time at all, she was snoring gently, breathing deeply, drained by the exertions of her earlier swim.

There was no moon, the cloudless sky was full of stars and the sea was like black glass. Scott began to feel insecure again.

He remembered staying at his gran's house in the country, sleeping way up in an attic overlooking some stables. When he'd felt alone, scared by the shadows from the yard lights, he'd listened to the horses snuffling and neighing, and he'd felt better. Here, he felt alone, full of responsibility for his sister.

They *had* to be close to land, surely? Scott gazed about the dark sea and felt very shaky. He remembered the shark they'd seen from the helicopter on the first day of their holiday and the feeling he'd had, dangling his feet over the stern of the *Carolina*. He suddenly imagined the great jaws crunching the raft in a single bite. In the quiet darkness, broken only by the wash of the sea, his imagination was running riot.

He turned his eyes away from the dark shadows of the water, glanced to his right – and jolted upright, seizing his binoculars.

There *was* a faint line of lights to the north.

And it was moving. It was something big. A cruise ship! But how far away? Five kilometres maybe?

There were two flares left: one orange smoke flare and a red star shell. Which way would the watch on the ship be looking? Ahead. Would anybody be looking over the side? A waiter having a cigarette? A passenger unable to sleep? Was it worth while?

His hand trembled as his finger closed on the trigger. One long-shot. Phut! the star shell was a dud! The orange container was a smoke flare, used in daytime only.

'No, no, no! *No!*'

'What's happening?' Gina sat up from where she had been sleeping.

Scott just pointed. 'The flare was a damned dud!' He slumped down.

Gradually the lights grew lower and lower on the horizon. Twenty minutes later, they were gone.

Scott felt very empty. Everything goes wrong for us, everything. Why? Why us? A couple of days ago we were eager for adventure, ready for the time of our lives. Now we are facing disaster.

I've got to do something, he thought, got to have something to focus on. He picked up the yellow emergency bag. I'll check how much stuff we've got left.

He couldn't sleep, so he began to rummage. Apart from what they had in their personal backpacks they had: eighteen pints of water (will last four or five days?), two unbreakable cups, one orange smoke flare, no red flares! (hopeless), one torch with spare bulbs and batteries, sweets one kilo (half eaten!), one Swiss Army knife with scissors, one compass, one tin of plasters, one mirror, a tube of sun cream factor 20, one fishing line and hooks, one strong nylon cord, one bag of dried fruit (eaten all but a handful), four energy bars, five tins of fruit (had been eight) plus tin-opener, two bananas …

Gina sat up. 'Why are you checking those packs? Don't you think we'll make land soon?' Now fear as well as fatigue showed in her eyes.

'Sure,' he said. 'I just want to know exactly

what we've got to eat. I've gone right off fruit and energy bars.'

'My watch now. You rest,' she offered.

Scott was asleep before his head hit his makeshift pillow.

His mind floated away. He was at school, scoring the winning basket. Then he was jet skiing with Cy, blasting along in the lead. But, halfway through the race, someone grabbed him by the arm. He tried to shake them off but it was no good.

'Scott! *Scott!*' Gina's panicky voice came crashing through his dream.

'What? What?' he mumbled.

'There's a light dead ahead!'

Scott took his big torch and pointed it at a white pin-point of light, way over the water. He waved his torch, but the light did not wave back. He didn't know Morse code. He remembered that the raft itself had an orange light on it, so maybe someone would see that?

The distant light was moving from right to left. After about fifteen minutes, it vanished. Had someone switched their light off on purpose? Had the other people gone behind a rock or an island?

Scott crouched by the raft opening, peering

intently towards the last position of the white light. It did not reappear.

Gina lay back disappointedly. Scott propped himself up. This was no time to doze.

A large black shadow loomed ahead. Scott didn't tell Gina yet; he wanted to be sure. He wanted no false jubilation. Now the raft was leaping, bumping up and down, and the water outside was rougher. There was a white line of foam coming fast. Land? Could it be land at last? The shadow grew; its shape became clearer. There were trees!

'Gina!' he shouted at last.

'What?' Gina yelled.

Before he could reply he heard the thunder of a speedboat's engine getting closer and closer. Scott tried to look round behind the raft. What he saw froze him completely: the brilliant headlight of the speeding craft was zooming towards him at an incredible pace.

'Hold on! We're going to be ...' Scott started to say, when the raft was hit by the massive wake and he was hurled into the white churning foam of the ocean.

He felt as though he was choking. Was he drowning?

Something was tangled round his neck, strangling him. The binoculars!

Gasping for breath as he surfaced, he yanked at the strap and felt the pressure slacken. Then the foamy swell swept him into hard coral which sliced into his shin, spinning him forward until other razor edges hit his forehead, his arms and legs, and then he tumbled free into dark water, swimming for his life.

CHAPTER THIRTEEN

Scott struggled blindly to the surface.

He tried to calm down. His heart was pounding. He trod water and jerked his head from side to side, trying to find his bearings. There was a white blur ahead of him and a dark mass above that. Land, yes! It had to be land! Swimming across twenty metres of lagoon seemed to take an age after the battering he had just received. He swung his leaden arms but could barely kick with his legs.

Then his feet touched something solid. Yes, there was sand – lovely, white sugary sand running between his toes. He had never felt anything so wonderful. Land, yes, land! He resisted the tug of the water and collapsed on the shore.

First, there was enormous relief – then a terrible feeling of loss.

Gina wasn't close by. Where was she?

'Gina! Gina!' he called.

'Over here!' She sounded some distance away and he couldn't see her.

'Are you … all right?' he shouted as normally as possible, realizing that his voice sounded more like a croak.

'Yes. I'm over here!'

Then he saw Gina walking unsteadily along the beach at the edge of the surf towards him. With her help he scrabbled clear of the water and then he lay, looking up at the massive, star-filled sky. Safe! At last! There was solid ground under his feet again.

'Scott. Your face is covered in blood!' Gina gasped.

He made a feeble attempt to stop it dripping into his eyes. 'I don't care! We've *made* it, Gina! Finally, we've made it!' he gasped.

For a while, they didn't say anything more. Nothing needed saying. Scott felt so good, no matter how bad his injuries were. His right leg felt numb. Even his head didn't hurt – yet. The excitement of the moment took away the immediate pain. Gina quickly removed her life-jacket so that she was free to help him. She retrieved her pack, which had drifted ashore, and pressed cotton wool from her waterproof first-aid kit to the gash on his forehead until the bleeding stopped.

Scott felt all the tension that had coiled up inside him release like the spring of a clock, and he lay back to bask in the sound of the rhythmic swish of the surf.

He was alive!

Then he slipped into sleep.

Scott woke to the smell of something burning. He opened his eyes. It was still dark, but he figured it must be before midnight; he didn't feel like he'd been asleep for long.

He found himself lying by a fire. Gina's handiwork, of course. He saw his backpack lying in the glow and wondered what else she'd salvaged from the raft.

He tried to move his head, but it hurt a lot. A bandage protected the wound. His right leg felt numb and stiff, and it was also bandaged. He was glad he'd been wearing the bulky life-jacket; it had protected his body when the life-raft had capsized. With an effort he sat up to look at his watch. It was just a blur. He held it up close to his face. It was just after 10 p.m.

Where was Gina?

Footsteps led away to the left but did not return. It was hard for him to scan the beach. Every movement sent spikes of pain through his body. There was no sign of Gina.

When his eyes had focused a little better, he noticed orange shreds of raft at the water's edge.

He looked around. Where are we?

He tried to stand up, but his bad leg folded and he fell down again. His fall left him on his back and facing a tree on the edge of the shallow beach. Suddenly he saw what it was that might have attracted Gina's attention. There was a small gap in the trees, almost level with where he was lying. Through the gap he could see distant treetops lit by a faint flickering glow. Another fire?

That's where she'll have gone. To investigate it.

Scott should have felt optimistic. He should have been cheered by the possibility of rescue, but his pain and all the other misfortunes of the trip had made him pessimistic. What if this island was the next rendezvous for the smugglers?

He felt terrible. His right leg was dead and

his forehead felt ready to split. His skin felt as if it had been shredded by sandpaper. His neck hurt too, and he wondered why – until he remembered the choking strap of his binoculars.

Scott took a couple of painkillers out of Gina's first-aid pack and gulped them down with a mouthful of warm water.

Half an hour passed. Bad leg or not, it was time to go looking for her. Scott couldn't stand the wait any longer.

He dragged himself over to some loose driftwood and chose a long enough piece that he thought would take his weight as a crutch. Then he hauled himself up and, with a massive effort, hobbled halfway across the beach before slumping down again.

A couple of minutes later, he gritted his teeth and had another go.

The beach was terrible to negotiate. His crude support was sinking deep into the silky soft sand, but at least he knew he was heading in the right direction, as Gina's footprints were quite easy to follow. The fifty or so metres to the nearest rocks took him five minutes but they felt like a marathon. He was soaking with sweat as he sat down and his heart was thundering.

Sheesh! he thought. It's going to take me for ever to get anywhere in this state! He wasn't used to feeling helpless, and he didn't like it.

Then he came to solid ground and a path under the trees. He saw the light of the fire again through the trees up ahead. A great rocky outcrop jutted out like a huge camel's hump into the sea. The beach with this new fire lay on the other side of the rock. Smoke swirled and wood sparks rose like fireflies into the dark night sky.

Scott started to hobble cautiously off the path and into the undergrowth, then he stopped. Someone was standing in the shadows watching him. He stared nervously into the darkness, but it was only Gina and she crept out towards him.

'You all right?' she whispered.

Scott nodded.

She pointed in the direction of the smoke. 'Some sort of party. Two boats. About ten men.'

'Well, let's go!' Scott's face lit up.

'But you said to be careful.'

'And?'

'When I got to the rocks I could hear them talking about hiding something. They were talking about "somebody coming", somebody who'd be "long gone by tomorrow". I didn't know what to do.'

'What boats have they got?'

'A catamaran and a red powerboat.'

'The same people who ignored us?' Scott asked.

'I don't know. I could only see two of the people on the beach properly. Neither of them was the man in the powerboat.'

Scott's inclination was to go straight in and ask for help. However, *that* was the old Scott. It would be too terrible to end up in deep trouble at the last hurdle after all they'd been through. He was also concerned that he wouldn't be able to make a run for it if things turned nasty.

'What are they doing?'

'Ten minutes ago they were drinking and cooking fish,' she said.

Lighting huge fires to attract attention didn't sound like the kind of thing drug smugglers went in for, Scott thought.

'Maybe we should go for it?' His sight was blurring again. He was feeling very ragged now.

'Earlier on,' Gina said, 'they brought some boxes ashore and hid them. I told you, they're waiting for someone.'

Scott felt his spirits drop.

Maybe it makes sense for smugglers to behave like this, he thought. Instead of creeping around, they light a fire, have a cook-in on a beach. It makes a good cover-story: anybody passing can see that it's party time.

'I want to take a look myself,' he said.

'Are you *sure*?'

'Yeah!' he said, gritting his teeth.

Scott hopped towards the rocks with Gina lending a hand. They could hear the sound of happy laughter. It really was party time. They turned right on to the promontory.

Scott and Gina edged along a rock that hid them from the men. There was a smooth shelf about twenty metres long running towards the sea, then curving in to the cove. Once again, excitement took the edge off Scott's pain. Quite close to the end, he saw that there was a deep V-shaped cleft that gave him a narrow view of the beach.

He couldn't see the fire, but right in his field of vision was a powerful-looking guy in blue shorts and a red shirt who said to someone out of view, 'It's good stuff. Enrique will like it!'

Good stuff? Scott sat up, alert to danger now. Then there was a new sound – another big powerboat.

Scott craned over to watch its approach. The great silver craft came skimming out of the darkness from the west. Scott leaned out even further. Gina reached to support him, but it was too late.

His right leg gave way and he slithered down the rocky cleft, to plunge towards the clear water.

'Scott!' Gina hissed helplessly as she watched him fall into the water below.

CHAPTER FOURTEEN

Scott wasn't a graceful diver at the best of times; his body, stiffened by injury, hit the surface like a slab of concrete.

For a split second he heard the shouts of the men and the cry of 'Scott!' from Gina. Then he was under the clear water, flapping clumsily like a stricken whale. Every desperate stroke was a wild lunge, but then he found both his right and left arms being seized by helping hands.

In the broken jigsaw of the swirl he caught a glimpse of Gina's green shorts and orange top at his side. Then he broke the surface, gulped down air and found himself held on the other side by an anxious-looking black man wearing stylish dreadlocks.

Scott saw Gina glance from side to side in case there was further danger. 'Help us, my brother's hurt!' she said as more men came forward to help Scott out of the water.

Scott tried to focus on their faces, but they all seemed to melt before his tired eyes and he sank to the sand.

'Our yacht sank. Scott got hurt on a reef!' Gina said, looking around anxiously. Fortunately all the men's faces showed concern, not aggression.

The white powerboat boomed into the cove and cruised to a halt behind them.

'Well,' the man with the dreadlocks said, 'you sure picked the right party to bust into. I'm a doctor. I'm Thomas.'

'Hey,' one of the others said, '*I'm* a doctor too!'

'Me too!'

Scott didn't laugh. 'Is this some sort of joke?'

'No joke,' a deep voice behind him boomed. Scott turned to see an elegant, athletic man in a black Armani T-shirt and shorts. 'I'm a doctor. Leaving here tomorrow to work in Houston. This is my leaving party!'

Gina gave Scott a hug. 'We're safe now! We've made it!'

Scott felt stunned. It was over, finally over. He slumped on to one of the floats of the beached yellow catamaran and held his bad leg.

'Let me have a look at you,' the tall man said. 'I'm Doctor Enrique Anderson, and bones are my speciality.'

Enrique worked quickly but gently, first removing the bandages, then feeling the line of Scott's shin, getting him to move his toes and testing how much sensation there was in his foot.

'How bad is it?' Scott asked.

'There could be a hairline fracture, but nothing's out of line.'

'But he says it's numb, and it's so swollen.' Gina wasn't reassured by the doctor's words.

'We need an X-ray, but don't worry, you'll live to shoot a few more hoops yet!'

Scott laughed.

Thomas appeared at Enrique's side and pointed to the other doctor.

'I tell you. If you're talking about bones … *he's the man!*'

Enrique turned to the rest of the party. 'Well, folks, you'd better start without me. I've got to make sure our friend here is OK.'

Thomas and Enrique helped Scott and Gina on board their small, sleek yacht, raised the anchor and set the white powerboat skimming across the dark waters towards distant lights.

'Thank you so much for helping us,' Gina said.

'Yes, thank you!'

'That's OK, guys.' Enrique smiled.

Scott lay back on a comfortable seat. He felt all the tension of their ordeal ooze out of his body.

An hour later, he was watching the lights grow closer and the great shadow of the volcano towering above Beef Island airport.

Thoughts of Clancy and Orlando sprang into his mind. Scott had been so afraid of trouble, so afraid of not making it, that he had focused exclusively on his own and Gina's survival.

'Can you check if my uncle, Clancy Stone, and our friend Orlando have been found? Our boats got separated.'

Enrique tried the hospital on his mobile phone, but he had difficulty in getting through. The coastguards also seemed to be busy.

'No go. Busy,' he said. 'We'll be there soon anyway.'

Fifteen minutes later, they cruised into port.

Before they docked, Gina shouted out. 'Look, Scott, there!'

A red powerboat was caught in a bright spotlight. A coastguard powerboat hemmed it in.

'That's why they didn't help!' Scott said. 'Bad news – I told you so!'

A minute afterwards, they tied up almost opposite the hospital. 'Hey,' a paramedic said as Enrique helped Scott into the building, 'I thought you'd left, doc!'

'So did I!' said Enrique.

Within minutes of landing, Scott was under an X-ray machine. They checked him out all over. He'd taken quite a few knocks on the boat, as well as the big hit from the rocks – and it showed.

While they waited for the results, Scott looked across at Gina as she chatted to Enrique. He thought of her big swim to the red powerboat, her taking care of him on the empty beach, and her determination on the island. Other little things became evident. He saw that she had a plaster on her arm, partly hidden by her T-shirt. Another above her knee. Then his vision started to go foggy again. It had needed both of them to get through. Neither could have survived alone.

Fifteen minutes after the X-ray, Dr Enrique's colleague came up to Scott, who was sitting in a wheelchair.

'Well, Scott, you're not going to win any beauty contests today, but nothing's broken. You are one tough sailor.'

'What about Uncle Clancy?' Scott said.

Dr Anderson turned to the radiographer. 'You see anything of a Mr … Stone, head injury?'

'Oh, yes,' the radiologist said. 'Found adrift off Anegada. The coastguard brought him in earlier on.'

'Serious?' Scott asked.

'No, no skull fracture, but I think they kept him in for observation – he was confused. That local guy wasn't so lucky – broken ribs, right arm, burns. Not sure how he's doing. They *might* have flown him to San Juan in Puerto Rico. I've only just come on duty.'

Scott still wasn't happy about the news. He wanted to see for himself. 'Can I see Clancy? I really need to!' he insisted.

Dr Enrique spoke to a colleague. When he returned he was smiling slightly.

'No problem about that. You'll be in the same ward for a day or two. We're keeping you in for observation as well.'

★

Gina wheeled Scott along a quiet corridor and they entered a small ward. They were both apprehensive about what they would find. Was Clancy really clear of danger? After all they'd been through, they had to see with their own eyes that everything was all right.

When they entered the ward, Clancy was on the phone. His face was bruised and he looked about a hundred years old. However, his mouth was working quite well again.

'Marie! Marie!' Clancy said, his eyes misting. 'They're here! Scott and Gina are here!'

Gina slid Scott alongside him.

'Quick, it's your mom!' Clancy said.

Scott snatched up the phone eagerly. 'Hi, Mom!'

'Hi, son. I believe that you've had some rough weather down there,' she said.

Scott raised an eyebrow. '*Rough weather!*'

Clancy was mouthing, 'Don't say anything!' Clearly he hadn't told their mom all the shocking details of their ordeal.

'That's right, Mom,' Scott said. 'But you know the sea …'

'Pity the boat was damaged,' she went on.

Clancy was now flapping like an eagle.

'Yes, Mom, but we're OK. It was *wild*! Here, talk to Gina.'

'Did you get any good photos?'

'Yes, Mom, I've taken three films already,' Gina said, trying to control her voice. 'There was this great reef with all these parrot fish, every colour of the rainbow. And ... yes ... did Scott do ... chores?' Scott gave her a thumbs-up. 'Of course ... he was as keen as ever!' Scott pulled a face and Gina grinned.

Clancy got back on the line.

'Well, Marie. We lost a bit of gear with the *Carolina*, so we won't be clear of here for ...' he looked up. Enrique was signalling 'five' with his fingers '... maybe five days, after the insurance paperwork is sorted out. OK. Ring tomorrow. Love you too.'

Then Mom rang off and it was just the three of them.

'The radiographer said that poor Orlando has broken ribs as well as burns.' Scott got right down to it.

But before Clancy could say anything, a weak voice cut across the conversation.

'Hey! Hey!' said the voice. 'What's with all this "*poor Orlando*" jive? I ain't dead yet!'

'Orlando!' Scott shouted, and Gina pushed

him over to the bandaged figure across the ward. 'We thought you were so bad that they'd flown you off to San Juan.'

'No way. Not for a few ribs. We both looked kind of messy when we got picked up off the dinghy by that fishing boat. We couldn't get a search going because it was only a rough catamaran, some local kid. Neither of us made any sense for a while.'

'You can't keep a good man down, though, eh, Orlando?' Clancy was grinning across.

'Yeah, and I tell you what, Mr Stone,' Orlando began, 'if you want a crewman to go shark fishing up Bermuda way any time soon …'

Gina looked at Scott. Scott looked at Clancy. Clancy looked at Orlando and then back at Scott.

'… then *forget it, man!*'

They all cracked up laughing, especially Orlando.

There was nothing else to say.

But their faces all said the same thing: never again, never *ever* again!

OCEAN TERROR

THE ESSENTIAL SURVIVAL GUIDE

Seas and oceans may seem inviting and friendly
on a beach during a summer holiday,
but beware ... A calm sea can change in no time
and a stormy sea can devastate your boat, no
matter how big it may be.

The seas and oceans can threaten you in a
number of different ways:

Giant waves can pound your vessel making
navigation difficult and the risk of
capsize very real

●

Your solid vessel can be turned into something
fragile and vulnerable

●

Sea fogs can make it almost impossible to see,
greatly increasing the risk of collision

●

Hidden offshore reefs can hole and sink your craft

●

Immersion in cold sea water after abandoning
ship can cause loss of the senses in a very
short period of time

●

If abandoning ship in warmer waters, you risk
putting yourself at the mercy of sharks, jellyfish
and even giant squid

THE OCEAN ALWAYS WINS!

Warnings

Most areas of the world issue hazard warnings for adverse sea and ocean weather. The best way to receive timely weather information is by radio.

Gale and storm warnings are broadcast at the first available programme junction and on the first news bulletin after receipt. Emergency messages are broadcast immediately on receipt.

You will be told what type of storm is on its way, including the strength and direction of the wind and roughly when it is expected:

> **Imminent** (less than six hours)
> **Soon** (between six and twelve hours)
> **Later** (twelve or more hours)

High winds, rough water and thunderstorms can suddenly turn a pleasant holiday outing into a frightening experience. When you prepare to embark, you should be aware of the current forecast and be able to receive warnings and weather advisories while underway.

Also, use your eyes! Keep watching the skies and look to the horizon for any build-up of unfriendly looking clouds.

Be Prepared!

The skipper is responsible for the safety of the boat and everyone on board. He or she must ensure that:

● The boat is suitable in design and construction for her intended journey

● The boat is in good condition

● The crew is competent and sufficiently strong

● The necessary safety and emergency equipment is on board

● The equipment is in good condition and the crew knows how to use it

Take nothing for granted. Test safety procedures regularly and insist that crew members wear life-jackets and harnesses when necessary (and that they clip on to safety lines). Make sure a lookout is maintained at all times. Listen to every forecast. Double-check all navigational calculations.

Boats require different sets of minimum safety equipment by International Law. These vary according to the size of the boat, type of propulsion, whether the vessel is operated at night or in periods of reduced visibility, and, in some cases, the body of water on which it is used.

You should not leave port without:

**Personal Flotation
Devices** – Life jackets.
You must carry one life
jacket in good condition
for each person on board.
Each must be in an
accessible location.

**Coastguard-approved
Fire Extinguishers**
The correct number of approved fire extinguishers,
depending on the size of boat, must be readily
available for use.

Visual Distress Signals
Most boats must be equipped with visual distress
signals designed for day use only, night use only
and combined day/night use.

Sound Signalling Devices
During periods of reduced visibility, you may need
to attract attention or sound fog signals. Boats of
twelve metres or more in length must carry a
whistle and a bell.

Emergency Position-indicating Radio Beacon
When activated, an EPIRB will transmit an
emergency signal that is picked up by satellites
and transmitted to rescue services. It should be
carried on any ocean journeys.

Liferafts

A rigid or inflatable life raft should be considered mandatory for anyone who cruises offshore.

It is also recommended that you carry additional safety equipment such as:

● Anchor with sufficient line or chain

● Bilge pump or bailer (bucket)

● First-aid kit

● VHF radio

● Extra fuel and water

● Tool kit

● Waterproof flashlight

● Compass

● Up-to-date charts for the area

● Man-overboard lifebouy (with light)

● Strong towing warp

MAYDAY!

If your vessel became unsafe or was about to founder, you would have to abandon it as quickly, efficiently and as safely as possible.

Sending a Mayday Message

MAYDAY is the most serious distress call. It takes priority over all other transmissions. Anybody in the crew should know how to pass a distress message, but this must only be done on the orders of the skipper and if the vessel or a person is in serious danger, requiring immediate assistance.

You should transmit:

– MAYDAY MAYDAY MAYDAY
– THIS IS (name of boat, spoken three times)
– MAYDAY (name of boat and personal call sign spoken once)
– MY POSITION IS (latitude and longitude, or true bearing and distance from a known point)
– Nature of distress (whether sinking, on fire, etc)
– Aid required
– Number of people on board
– Any other important, helpful information (eg, if the boat is drifting, whether distress rockets are being fired)
– OVER

Mayday is the representation of the French words *m'aider*, meaning 'help me'.

ABANDON SHIP!

Before abandoning ship for the lifeboat or a raft, you should try to:

Dress in warm clothing. Wear sweaters underneath your wet weather jackets. Fasten your life jacket back on top. Keep extra clothes in a nearby bag.

Fill containers three-quarters full of fresh water from on-board supplies. They will float in the sea because of the air bubble inside.

Collect together any fresh food, tins and tin openers.

Collect up navigation gear, a waterproof torch, extra flares, a bucket, length of line and a first-aid kit.

After abandoning ship, you should try to:

Huddle together for warmth.

Construct a shelter on the raft.

Keep a good lookout for ships and aircraft.

Ration fresh water to half a litre per person each day. (Do not drink seawater or urine. Either will dehydrate you.)

Collect rain water. Plastic or polythene is best for collecting dew and rain.

Take sea-sickness pills. Being sick will quickly leave you dehydrated and weak.

Use flares sparingly. If potential rescuers are five or more miles away use red rocket 'parachute' flares. If they are nearer, use orange smoke flares in daylight hours and red handheld flares at night.

Set off flares in pairs. A single flare may be dismissed as an optical illusion.

Rescue!

A helicopter should be able to rescue you directly from your boat, provided that the sails have all been lashed down tightly, together with any loose gear on deck.

The crucial rules are:

1) Listen to the instructions of the helicopter pilot on VHF radio. He or she is in charge and will tell you if it is necessary to abandon the boat.

2) Allow the wire from the helicopter to 'earth' itself in the sea before bringing it – and probably the helicopter crewperson – on board your boat.

3) The boat must, if possible, be steered on an accurate course into the wind.

Ocean Storms – The Facts

How?
Tropical storms blow around an area of low pressure. The rotation of the wind around the eye of the storm is anti-clockwise in the northern hemisphere and clockwise in the southern hemisphere. Depending where they occur, these storms are known as hurricanes, cyclones, typhoons or willy-willies.

When?
Tropical storms are most frequent during late

Area	Season
West Indies	June–November
NE Pacific	May–November
NW Pacific	All year
Bay of Bengal	May–December
Arabian Sea	April–December
S Indian	November–May
S Pacific	November–April

summer or early autumn in both hemispheres. The only tropical area entirely free of hurricanes is the South Atlantic. In the North-west Pacific, no month is considered to be entirely safe, although typhoons are extremely rare in winter.

Effect?
Any boat lying in the path of a storm, particularly the centre of the storm, is in serious danger. The extremely strong winds generated by these storms and the huge seas they raise can easily overwhelm a boat.

Where?
The tropical storm seasons around the world are:

Highest frequency

September

July–September

July–October

October– November

April–May, October–November

December–April

January–March

11

Stormy Weather

The strength of wind is measured by the Beaufort scale, which ranges from force one to force twelve. Anything force six or below is considered to be nothing more than a strong wind, and of concern only to small boats.

The state of the sea and probable wave heights are a guide as to what may be expected in the open sea, away from land. In enclosed waters, or near land with an offshore wind, wave heights will be less but the waves may possibly be steeper!

1	2	3	4	5	6	7	8	9	10	11	12

Force 7   Near gale
Probable wave height – 4 metres
Windspeed – 52–62 km/h (28–33 knots)
Sea heaps up; white foam from breaking waves begins to blow in streaks

1	2	3	4	5	6	7	8	9	10	11	12

Force 8   Gale
Probable wave height – 5.5 metres
Windspeed – 63–75 km/h (34–40 knots)
Moderately high waves of greater length; the edge of crests break into spindrift; foam is blown in well-marked streaks

| 1 | 2 | 3 | 4 | 5 | 6 | 7 | 8 | 9 | 10 | 11 | 12 |

Force 9   Severe gale
Probable wave height – 7 metres
Windspeed – 76–88 km/h (41–47 knots)
High waves with tumbling crests; dense streaks of
foam; spray may affect visibility

| 1 | 2 | 3 | 4 | 5 | 6 | 7 | 8 | 9 | 10 | 11 | 12 |

Force 10   Storm
Probable wave height – 9 metres
Windspeed – 89–103 km/h (48–55 knots)
Very high waves with long overhanging crests;
dense streams of foam make surface of sea
white; heavy tumbling sea; visibility affected

| 1 | 2 | 3 | 4 | 5 | 6 | 7 | 8 | 9 | 10 | 11 | 12 |

Force 11   Violent storm
Probable wave height – 11 metres
Windspeed – 104–117 km/h (56–63 knots)
Exceptionally high waves; sea completely cover-
ed with long white patches of foam; edge of wave
crests blown into froth; visibility affected

| 1 | 2 | 3 | 4 | 5 | 6 | 7 | 8 | 9 | 10 | 11 | 12 |

Force 12   Hurricane
Probable wave height – 14 metres
Windspeed – 118+ km/h (64+ knots)
Air filled with foam and spray; sea completely
white with driving spray; visibility very seriously
affected

GPS

GPS stands for Global Positioning System. Using a GPS receiver you can determine your location anywhere in the world with great precision. It operates at anytime, in any weather, anywhere. There are twenty-four GPS satellites – operated by the United States Department of Defense – in orbit above the Earth. These are continuously monitored by ground stations located worldwide.

GPS provides two levels of service. Standard Positioning Service (SPS) and Precise Positioning Service (PPS).

SPS is available to all GPS users and provides positioning accuracy within 100 metres horizontally and 156 metres vertically.

PPS is available to US and Allied military, certain US Government agencies and selected civil users specifically approved by the US Government. It has a twenty-two-metre horizontal accuracy and a 27.7 metre vertical accuracy.

EPIRB

An EPIRB is an Emergency Position-indicating Radio Beacon – a search and rescue device that transmits a radio signal on specific emergency frequencies. The radio transmission provides a means by which search-and-rescue forces can locate the emergency.

Satellite EPIRBs transmit a digital message to a satellite, allowing identification of a particular vessel when that EPIRB is registered. Registration of an EPIRB is compulsory and is updated annually. Information on country registration, captain and call sign is included, as well as position anywhere on the earth's surface to an accuarcy of less than five kilometres. The message is retransmitted to local ground stations around the globe, then on to a Rescue Co-ordination Centre for deployment of search-and-rescue services.

A 400mhz EPIRB device

Ocean Disasters – The Biggies

Place: Atlantic Ocean
Date: 14 April 1912
Vessel: *Titanic*
Death toll: 1,503

There are few people who have not heard the name *Titanic* and don't know of her disasterous end. Considered 'unsinkable' by some, the White Star Liner sank after hitting an iceberg in the Atlantic Ocean – just five days after she left Southampton on her maiden voyage in 1912. More than 1,500 lives were lost that night. Tragically, the death toll might not have been so high had more lifeboats been provided. The subject of countless books, films, documentaries and exhibitions – interest in the *Titanic* was fuelled when a deep-sea exploration team headed by Dr Robert Ballard discovered the rusted, shattered wreck on the seabed in 1985.

Place: St Lawrence River
Date: 29 May 1914
Vessel: *Empress of Ireland*
Death toll: 1,012

The *Empress of Ireland* was bound for Liverpool, England when it sailed away from her berth in Quebec Harbour for her first voyage of the summer. Only hours into her voyage, she collided with the Norwegian collier, *Storstad*, and sank in the gulf of the St Lawrence River. The ships had actually spotted each other when they were three miles apart but confusing signals, altered courses and thick fog led to disaster. The icy waters reached the engines in three minutes, and the *Empress of Ireland* sank within fourteen minutes. The Captain survived, despite remaining on the bridge as the *Empress* sank beneath him. He was able to present his account of events to a court investigating the tragedy. The First Officer was found negligent for not informing his Captain of the incoming fog.

Place: Baltic Sea
Date: 30 January 1945
Vessel: *Wilhelm Gustloff*
Death toll: 5,400

A converted 25,000-ton luxury liner, the *Wilhelm Gustloff*, had been serving as a hospital ship when it left the Baltic harbour of Gydnia jammed with nearly 5,000 refugees – mostly women and children – and 1,600 military service-men. At shortly after nine o'clock in the evening, it was struck by three torpedoes from Soviet submarine S–13. Convey vessels were able to rescue only 900 people from the sub-freezing waters.

Place: Liaodong Wan & East China Sea
Date: 1948
Vessel: Unidentified Troopship and *Kiangya*
Death toll: 6,000 and 3,000

China suffered two of the greatest losses of

human life ever known at sea in same year. In November 1948, whilst evacuating troops from Manchuria near Yankou, an unidentified Chinese Troopship sank in the Liaodong Wan Sea with the loss of an estimated 6,000 lives. Weeks later, the *Kiangya* passenger ship carrying refugees fleeing Communist troops struck an old mine, exploded and sank off the coast near Shanghai. Over 3,000 people are believed to have perished.

Place: Baltic Sea
Date: 28 September 1994
Vessel: The *Estonia* car ferry
Death toll: 757

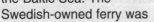

A design flaw and a slow response by the crew to signs of trouble were largely responsible for 1994's *Estonia* ferry disaster in which 757 people died in the rough waters of the Baltic Sea. The Swedish-owned ferry was on its way from Tallinn, Estonia to Stockholm in Sweden when the bow doors were jolted open causing the ship to take on water and eventually sink. The accident shocked many people by its size, speed and because this type of ship had been thought to be completely safe.

Weird!

The strangest things happen at sea.

Off Japan, there exists a stretch of water known as the 'Devil' or 'Ghost' sea in which many ships, craft and aircraft have disappeared. Sudden tidal waves are common in the area. There are also reports of weird luminous 'white water' and holes or hills suddenly appearing in areas of the sea!

In 1959 two rescue boats went to help a vessel in trouble off the coast of Devon. It was identified as a military landing craft, flying the Cross of Lorraine – used only during the Second World War by the 'Free French'. As the two ships closed in, their view of the craft was hidden by a huge wave. They did not see the landing craft again. Many suspect it was a ghost ship from the 1940s ...

The ancient mummy case of Egyptian Princess Ammon-Ra, given to the British Museum, seemed to bring only bad luck and the Museum decided to get rid of it. It was arranged that the mummy case be sent to an American museum. The ship on which this unlucky object was loaded for its journey to America was ... the *Titanic*!